CU00961570

THE SOCIAL CONTEXT OF THEOLOGY

THE SOCIAL CONTEXT
OF THEOLOGY

A Methodological Enquiry

by

ROBIN GILL

DURHAM COUNTY LIBRARY

ACC. No. 2054160

CLASS No. 261

MOWBRAYS
LONDON AND OXFORD

© Robin Gill

ISBN   0   264   66019   6

First published in 1975 by A. R. Mowbray & Co. Ltd.,
The Alden Press, Osney Mead, Oxford OX2 OEG

Text set in 11/12 pt. Modern, printed by letterpress, and bound in Great Britain
at The Pitman Press, Bath

Preface

As a human activity theology should be of interest to the specialist of social interactions, the sociologist. In so far as it is a human activity theologians ought to listen to the sociologist. These are the twin contentions of this methodological enquiry into the social context of theology. Curiously, they may appear highly prosaic to some, whilst dangerously reductionist to others.

In fact, the abundance of unfounded assumptions that theologians tend to make about the nature of contemporary society suggests that the social context of theology is worth considering. Others, of course, have bemoaned these assumptions, but they have seldom attempted to explore them in any systematic way. I will argue in Part 2 of this book in particular, that a thoroughly rigorous analysis is long over-due in this area.

Both sociologists and theologians may detect elements of reductionism at various stages of my argument. The former may consider that I have effectively reduced the sociological perspective to the status of a handmaid of theology: the latter may be convinced that I have reduced theology to no more than a human activity—precluding the role of the Holy Spirit from theology. These charges of reductionism must be taken seriously—especially in view of the uncharted nature of this interdisciplinary territory—and I will examine them at length in Part 1 of this book.

If I were to be asked to review this book (a monstrous eventuality) I would suggest that Chapters 5 and 9 are especially vulnerable.

The latter offers an alternating model of secularisation and de-secularisation as one means of depicting the social context of theology. It concludes a lengthy discussion in Part 3 of sociological defenders of a *thoroughgoing* secularisation model and sociological critics of *any* secularisation model. As a model it remains relatively unexplored in the context of theology—as indeed it must in a methodological, rather than substantive,

v

enquiry. Hopefully, though, I will be able to pursue its specifically theological implications at a future date—its consequences for the peculiarly theological problems or theodicy and verification I believe to be particularly important.

Chapter 5 is clearly indebted to some of Professor Berger's notions from the sociology of knowledge. Whether or not I have been faithful to these (I may well have expanded them somewhat), my argument is especially vulnerable to a sophisticated caricature. The latter may be crudely expressed as follows; theology can *never* communicate apart from contemporary plausibility structures, therefore the latter must *always* dictate the former: the result is that the world re-writes the Gospel in every generation and theology can *never* sit in judgement on current societal assumptions no matter how fallacious they might be.

I hope to refute this caricature in my next book on the social structure of theology. In some ways the present work is offered as a prelude to it. An examination of the social structure of theology—a much-needed, but again astonishingly unresearched, area of sociological enquiry—suggests the very real possibility that theology may at times act as an independent, and not simply as a dependent, variable within society. In theological terms, theology may indeed sit in judgement on conventional wisdom on occasions—as a matter of empirical fact.

A book is never the product of a single moment of writing, and I am immensely indebted to all those who helped me as a post-graduate, first in theology and then in sociology, and to all those colleagues who continue to help me now. Through them I am increasingly discovering that the two disciplines are by no means mutually exclusive—even sharing unexpected aspirations at times. In the particular task of preparing the various drafts of this book, though, I was supported, encouraged and helpfully criticised by a number of academics. Professor David Martin of the London School of Economics read my initial draft and prodded it into its present shape. Dr Alastair Campbell of the Department of Christian Ethics and Practical Theology here at Edinburgh has patiently read most of my writings including the present one. Professor David Harned of the Department of Religious Studies at Virginia University has supplied me with detailed and immensely helpful criticisms of this work. And finally Dr Anthony Coxon of the Department of Sociology again at Edinburgh has read and criticised the completed draft. The faults, of course, are all mine and not theirs, but their criticisms have proved invaluable.

This book might have appeared much sooner, though considerably less enjoyably, had it not been for my family. For that I am extremely grateful.

ROBIN GILL

Foreword

In this book Robin Gill conducts an expert exploration into the relationships between sociology and theology. He does so with particular reference to the concept of secularisation since this is subject to debate in both disciplines. Basically he is arguing two points. One is that theologians utilise sociology, both implicitly and explicitly, but rarely pay sociology the courtesy of an extended acquaintance with what it has to offer. The other point is that what sociology has to offer is often ambiguous. Sociologists need to recognise this ambiguity and theologians need to be prepared to cope with it when employing sociological materials. This desideratum becomes particularly clear when dealing with large scale surveys of 'the secularisation process' whether over the last three hundred years – to select Hazard's formulation, or over the last three thousand years, as propounded by Peter Berger. The keynotes of our approach should be agnosticism and ambiguity.

The ambiguity is not immediately obvious or omnipresent. If, for example, you walk through the Academy in Venice you see that the sequence of paintings from the thirteenth century to the eighteenth tells the conventional secularisation story straight and plain. Yet open a book on the history of music up to the mid-twentieth century, and observe the immense religious works of the most contemporary composers. One is immediately plunged into ambiguity. Then visit an exhibition of English art over the last four hundred years and notice that there is very little religious art, at any point: such as there is (a Blake, a Watts or a Spencer) fits no easily discernible pattern. Examine Russian art and there is one sudden predominant shift: from Ikons to an art suffused by Enlightenment.

So much to illustrate ambiguity and diversity, but the illustrations given also underline a point crucial to this study. This concerns the varied histories of religious 'tone' to be found in different social sectors. Elite developments, the tendencies of the artistic and academic enclaves, and the broad religious currents of other status groups all proceed at different rates, and one cannot *assume* that any one sector leads the rest. Theologians are mostly ensconced in a specialised part of the intelligentsia and are peculiarly prone to project their own social experience onto 'modern man' at large. The notion of 'modern man' (like that of 'our modern secular society' or 'contemporary pluralism') then acquires the vigour of a pregnant cliché. The use of sociological materials by theologians often illustrates the power of pregnant cliché. Challenged by a demand for some element of *scientific* agnosticism your theologian easily becomes irritable. Social science has no right to be that complicated. And anyway the fascinating glimpse of a possible connection was too seductive to be overlaid by uncertainty.

It is all very understandable: the unconscious and hidden evolutionary assumptions of some sociologists, the intransigent dislike of sociology or the indiscriminate raiding of it by some theologians. Social science is long and life is short. Nevertheless the confusion and complication must be grappled with. Even our most cherished clichés may have to go: the autonomy of contemporary man for example. When we observe the operations of political ideology as a social system or the Kuhminan view of how science works as a social reality we can only note that men are bound and live by what binds. What once appeared exclusive to the social reality of religion now appears a general characteristic of social reality as such: masks and masquerades, bonds and boundaries, ritual communication and ex-communication, sects and sectarianisms, dogmatism and the casuistic evasion of doctrine for pragmatic motives.

The natural history of man's projections onto the universe and the possible correspondence of those projections with what is *there* each present complex tasks. Dr Gill's book is a preliminary essay in examining the links between both forms of complexity.

David Martin

Contents

PART ONE

Methodological Considerations

1

Three Sociological Approaches to Theology

As YET there is a rather thin body of literature on possible correlations between sociology and theology. With the notable exceptions of Peter Berger[1] in the States and David Martin[2] in Britain very few sociologists of religion have written on theological themes. Conversely, very few theologians have attempted any sophisticated form of co-operation with sociologists. In complete contrast to the immense body of literature devoted to the inter-relation of theology and philosophy, that concerned with theology and sociology is extraordinarily limited.

Doubtless there are many reasons for this state of affairs. The language barrier between the two disciplines may in part be responsible. Inevitably, both sociology and theology have constructed autonomous specialist terms which only those trained in sociology or theology are likely to understand. However, the situation is no different if one compares the languages of philosophy and theology. It should not in principle be too difficult for the competent theologian to acquire a certain measure of expertise in sociological terms, or for the sociologist to acquire a similar expertise in theological terms.

More crucially, though, the possibility of conflict may daunt some who might otherwise be inclined to explore relations and interactions between sociology and theology—or socio-theological correlations as I shall term such explorations for convenience. In the following chapters I will examine some of these conflicts, at both the methodological and empirical levels. However, it is as well to realise at this stage that such conflicts do exist, and that they may have dissuaded some from studying this largely uncharted area of scholarship.

Finally it should be pointed out that the attitude of some of the pioneer sociologists of religion was often construed by theologians as effectively 'anti-religious'—a quality not designed to endear sociologists to theologians. Certainly it was

3

known that few of the pioneer sociologists of religion were 'orthodox' Christians. Even Max Weber, as sympathetic towards religion as he was, by no means was 'orthodox' in his religiosity. Again, I shall return to this issue when I examine the role of explanation within both the sociology of religion and theology in Chapter 3.

This is not the place to map out in detail the reasons for the comparative neglect of possible socio-theological correlations. It is the place, though, to argue that such correlations are important, both for theology and for the sociology of religion. A recurrent theme throughout this book will be that this is a fruitful, but much neglected, area of scholarship.

In Part 2, in particular, I will be critical of some of the correlations that contemporary theologians have offered. I will argue that a far more sophisticated form of correlation is necessary if one is to do justice to both sociology and theology. However, it would have been equally possible to criticise some of the correlations that sociologists themselves have offered. To redress the balance somewhat two examples of inadequate correlation on the part of social theorists might be offered—the first by Ernst Troeltsch and the second by J. Milton Yinger.

Troeltsch's analysis of religious institutions[3] has become the seminal basis within much contemporary sociology of religion for accounts of Church/Sect typology (the study of differing types and dynamics within religious institutions). Today, of course, it is more usual to classify religious institutions in terms of Church, Denomination and Sect, rather than Troeltsch's Church, Sect and Mysticism. Nevertheless, the broad outline of his analysis has proved invaluable to the sociologist.

Troeltsch believed that the social structures of religious institutions are theologically rooted. He argued that the Church/Sect/Mysticism structure of the Christian Church was neither fortuitous nor simply the product of organizational pressure. Instead this structure is inherent in the Gospel itself, and, so long as Christianity survives, this triadic structure will also survive. Troeltsch believed that each type of structure complemented the other; the inclusive Church was strengthened by the exclusive Sect, and both were further strengthened by the individualistic Mysticism. The Church could offer objective grace, the Sect a community of love, and Mysticism individual

4

experience free from formalized worship and belief. Together these three types of structure could present to society differing, but complementary, facets of the Christian Gospel.

In view of the comparative importance of Troeltsch's typology within the sociology of religion, it is interesting that he offered this theological interpretation of his analysis. Nevertheless, it faces at least two important difficulties.

Firstly, contemporary sociologists, with their focus on religion in general rather than Christianity in particular, tend to argue that an adequate Church/Sect typology should be applicable to world religions. So, for example, both Roland Robertson[4] and Bryan Wilson[5] are careful to frame typologies which do not simply apply to Christianity. Wilson's seven-fold system of classifying Sects, in particular, introduces types which are at times only very marginally concerned with Christianity. It is possible that a typology which is too close to the Christian Gospel will prove inadequate in this wider context.

Secondly, contemporary sociologists tend to point to the confusion of criteria that is apparent in Troeltsch's typology. He employs several sets of criteria to determine whether or not a particular religious movement should be identified as Church, Sect or Mysticism. Sometimes these criteria are theological— for example, the predominance within a particular religious movement of certain theological models such as 'grace' or 'love'. At other times the criteria correspond more closely to current organisational theory—for example, the presence or absence of professional functionaries within a particular movement.

In reaction to this confusion sociologists like Demerath[6] have argued that almost any criteria are preferable to those which are theologically or religiously rooted. Typologies which are so rooted fit uneasily into general sociological theory and make comparative study difficult if not impossible: on the other hand, typologies based solely on organisational theory may provide a more adequate sociological foundation for further analysis.

Yinger also provides an interesting, though again inadequate, socio-theological correlation in the way he derives his functional definition of religion. He takes his initial cue from Tillich:

> Paul Tillich has said that religion is that which concerns us ultimately. This can be a good starting point for a functional

definition. While there are important disagreements concerning the 'ultimate' problems of man, a great many would accept the following as among the fundamental concerns of human societies and individuals: How shall we respond to the fact of death? Does life have some central meaning despite the suffering, the succession of frustrations and tragedies? . . .[7]

From this theological definition Yinger attempts a formal sociological definition of religion:

Religion, then, can be defined as a system of beliefs and practices by means of which a group of people struggles with these ultimate problems of human life. It is the refusal to capitulate to death, to give up in the face of frustration, to allow hostility to tear apart one's human association.[8]

I shall be returning to the complexities raised by functional definitions of religion in Chapter 8. At present, though, it should be noted that Yinger's dependence on Tillich is unfortunate. One of the important consequences of this dependence is that Yinger exposes himself to the same weaknesses as Tillich.

The philosopher H.D. Lewis describes Tillich's concept of 'ultimate concern as a confusing attenuation of faith . . . the standing temptation of liberal minded thinkers to gain recognition of Christian truth and adherents'.[9] For Lewis it is an attempt to claim that everyone is ultimately a Christian believer—'the only way in which we could make Tillich's statement plausible would be by identifying belief in God with seriousness'.[10] Similarly, the sociologist Betty Scharf argues that Yinger's definition 'is cast in wide terms which allow almost any kind of enthusiastic purpose or strong loyalty, provided it is shared by a group, to count as religion'.[11] Thus both Tillich and Yinger are criticised for the same reason; they allow almost any form of strongly-held ideology to count as religion. The weakness of this position should become more apparent later.

In contrast to these two attempts by sociologists to use theological concepts in the service of sociology, there are three basic sociological approaches to theology which might prove to be more adequate; a study of the social determinants of theological positions, a study of the social significance of theological positions and a study of the social context of theology.

There is a small, but growing, amount of interest amongst sociologists in the social determinants of moral ideas[12]—though this has traditionally been a pursuit of anthropologists rather than sociologists. In addition, the social determinants of specifically religious beliefs and practices have constantly been the preoccupation of sociologists of religion. But there has been comparatively little attention paid to the social determinants of theological positions as such. Yet it is quite clear that sociology, like psychology,[13] could play an important role in examining particular theological positions—though not, of course, the validity of these positions.

Theologians inevitably interact with society at large, and, however much they may seek to influence that society, they themselves are influenced by it. Peter Berger argues that this is necessarily the case:

> Sociology . . . raises questions for the theologian to the extent that the latter's positions hinge on certain socio-historical presuppositions. For better or for worse, such presuppositions are particularly characteristic of theological thought in the Judaeo-Christian orbit, for reasons that are well known and have to do with the radically historical orientation of the Biblical tradition. The Christian theologian is, therefore, ill-advised if he simply views sociology as an ancillary discipline that will help him (or, more likely, help the practical churchman) to understand certain 'external' problems of the social environment in which his church is related. . . . On strictly methodological grounds it will be possible for the theologian to dismiss this new perspective as irrelevant to his *opus proprium*. This will become much more difficult, however, as soon as he reflects that, after all, he was not born as a theologian, that he existed as a person in a particular socio-historical situation before he ever began to do theology—in sum, that he himself, if not his theology, is illuminated by the lighting apparatus of the sociologist.[14]

Berger's argument is thoroughly persuasive. Theology is written by theologians, and the latter are human beings living in a human society. This platitude carries the obvious implication that theologians, like all other thinkers and writers, *can* properly be examined by the sociologist.

The sociologist concerned to study the social determinants of theological positions might achieve this by examining either the work of a single theologian or a theological position in general. Adopting the first approach he might, for example, attempt to trace the influence of two world wars on the theology of Karl Barth, a factor any comprehensive analysis of the latter's work must take into consideration.[15] Very little sociological research has employed such analysis.

Adopting the second approach, the sociologist might, for example, be concerned to explore the influence of social structures on theological positions in general. Some of the research in the field of Church/Sect typology has indeed been concerned with just such an influence. At many points the socio-historical surveys of both Troeltsch[16] and Werner Stark[17] illustrate the social determinants of general theological positions. The latter's interpretation of the origin of Sects, in particular, provides an example of an attempt to use this approach:

> The last root of all sectarianism lies in the alienation of some group from the inclusive society within which it has to carry on its life. It is a kind of protest movement, distinguished from other similar movements by the basic fact that it experiences and expresses its dissatisfactions and strivings in religious (rather than political or economic or generally secular) terms. The causes of alienation can be many, but hunger and humiliation easily come first. All through history, the lowest ranks of society have been the prime recruiting ground of heresies and schisms.[18]

Bryan Wilson is less concerned with such sweeping historical generalisations than with a detailed study of contemporary Sects. Nevertheless, he too attempts to trace the varied social determinants of sectarian theology. His seven-fold typology of Sects is based on the single criterion of a Sect's 'response to the world'—a variable manifestly influenced by a Sect's theology. Wilson argues that this criterion 'recognises the ideological character of sects, without nevertheless neglecting the way of life of the sect's members, which also necessarily affect the manner in which they accept, reject, neglect or attempt to transcend, to improve or to transvaluate the opportunities which worldly society may offer'.[19]

8

Wilson's attempt to trace the social determinants of theological positions can also be seen in his account of the process of secularisation[20]—to which again I shall be returning in Chapter 7. He argues that current ecumenical theology within the Church acts as a 'new faith' within an overall situation of secularisation. Far from being a sign of strength within the Church, or a 'return to the Gospel', ecumenical theology is in fact a sign of organisational weakness and a product of the process of secularisation within the West.

Finally, Weber's interactionist approach to religion provides numerous examples of an attempt to establish the social determinants of theological concepts. His account of the rise of monotheism well illustrates this point:

> Among the Greeks, philosophers interpreted whatever gods were found elsewhere as equivalent to and so identical with the deities of the moderately organized Greek pantheon. This tendency towards universalization grew with the increasing predominance of the primary god of the pantheon, that is, as he assumed more of a 'monotheistic' character. The growth of a world empire in China, the extension of the power of the Brahmin caste throughout all the varied political formations in India, and the development of the Persian and Roman empires favoured the rise of both universalism and monotheism, though not always in the same measure and with quite different degrees of success.[21]

The rise of monotheism and universalism, then, is correlated by Weber with the rise of political imperialism.

A Study of the Social Significance of Theological Positions:

Whereas the first approach takes seriously the possibility that society has influenced theological positions, this approach suggests that the latter may at times influence society. An interactionist approach demands that both sociological approaches be treated as viable possibilities.

I have argued elsewhere[22] that theology has all too often been ignored as a possible independent variable in the sociology of religion. I attempted to show in the British context that both the debate centring around John Robinson's *Honest to God* in 1963 and the breakdown of the proposed Anglican/Methodist

Union in 1969 showed the possibility that theology itself could act as an independent religious variable. The *Honest to God* debate contained certain non-theological factors which may have influenced the general public in Britain at the time, whereas the breakdown of the proposed Union apparently defies most sociological theories of ecumenism and suggests that one should take seriously the possibility that specifically theological differences of opinion were a causal factor in it. Both of these examples indicated only a possibility—though I believe a possibility which demands a more serious attempt on the part of sociologists of religion to examine the role of theology vis à vis general religiosity.

The comparative neglect of this approach in contemporary sociology of religion is, perhaps, somewhat surprising in view of the importance that Weber placed on it. The latter's radical thesis in his *The Protestant Ethic and the 'Spirit' of Capitalism*, which first a‍ peared in 1905, suggested that one of the variables responsible in some way for the rise of capitalism in the West may have been Calvinist theology. In particular, Weber singled out the theological concepts of vocation, predestination, inner-worldly asceticism and sanctification as being of peculiar relevance to the rise of capitalism. Whatever criticisms may be made of this thesis,[23] it is important to realise that it is more modest than it is sometimes portrayed:

> We have no intention whatever of maintaining such a foolish and doctrinaire thesis as that the spirit of capitalism . . . could only have arisen as the result of certain effects of the Reformation, or even that capitalism as an economic system is a creation of the Reformation. In itself, the fact that certain important forms of capitalistic business organisation are known to be considerably older than the Reformation is a sufficient refutation of such a claim. On the contrary, we only wish to ascertain whether and to what extent religious forces have taken part in the qualitative formation and the quantitative expansion of that spirit over the world.[24]

Weber's thesis has been the object of a considerable amount of sociological research,[25] particularly since 1961, when Gerhard Lenski[26] claimed that it could be used as a contemporary model to explore current differences between Catholics and Protestants.

Gary Bauma, however, believes that much of the research which has used the Weberian thesis as a contemporary, rather than historical, model has been inadequately based. His main criticism of this research—a criticism that is highly relevant in the present context—is that it ignores important theological differences between Protestants. Bouma argues that the researchers 'did not check whether any of the people who are classified Protestant believed in predestination, viewed their jobs as a calling, felt as though they ought to do all for the glory of God, actually held ascetic norms, or felt it necessary to order their lives rationally . . . in the attempt to determine the effect of inner-worldly asceticism as contrasted with that of other-worldly mysticism, most researchers simply fell back on the assumption that Protestants are inner-worldly ascetics and Roman Catholics are other-worldly mystics.'[27]

One area, however, which has been comparatively well researched is that concerning a possible correlation between theology and racial prejudice. On the specific issue of anti-Semitism, Glock and Stark have claimed that there is a strong correlation between it and a high level of Christian 'orthodoxy'. In their major empirical study of 3,000 church members, however, they found no similar correlation between 'orthodoxy' and attitudes towards Black Americans. They eventually concluded that specifically theological notions, such as that of particularism, acted as independent variables within the area of anti-Semitism. They pictured the causal sequence as follows:

Orthodox faith that claims universal truth and specifies in detail what that truth is leads persons to take a particularistic conception of their religious status. They think of themselves as having a patent on religious virtue and hence discredit all persons who do not share in their faith. Particularism leads Christians to be especially negative in their historic image of ancient Jewry, to see the Jews as implicated in the Crucifixion of Jesus. The combination of these factors markedly predisposes Christians to hold a negative religious image of the modern Jew as unforgiven for the 'sins' of his ancient forebears, and suffering God's punishment.[28]

They do not, of course, claim that these theological factors are

11

either the sole cause or the sine qua non of anti-Semitism, but they do claim that they are important. Even this limited claim, however, is unlikely to appeal to theologians.

It is significant, perhaps, that both 'orthodoxy' and anti-Semitism appear to be higher amongst Sects than amongst Churches in the Glock and Stark survey. I shall argue in Chapter 7 that this is hardly surprising since their scale of 'orthodoxy' involves a somewhat sectarian understanding of religious 'certainty'. Nevertheless, even this observation does not destroy their claim that certain types (albeit sectarian) of theological concept predispose people towards anti-Semitism. There is, though, the claim of other researchers[29] that the predisposing factor is not so much Christian 'orthodoxy' as generalized dogmatism or authoritarianism. On this understanding, both sectarian 'orthodoxy' and anti-Semitism would have common roots in authoritarian attitudes.

A rather different way of approaching the possibility that theology may act at times as an independent sociological variable is suggested by Roderick Martin. After a brief analysis of Durkheim, Weber and Marx, he suggests that their work demonstrates the inseparability of social diagnosis and social research. Their concepts 'were initially presented as part of a critique of contemporary society that was often moral and ideological in origin'.[30] He believes this is particularly true of the concept of alienation in Marx, of that of disenchantment in Weber and of social disintegration in Durkheim. An adequate appreciation of pioneer sociology must see that 'it drew its theoretical concepts from sources as diverse as Christian theology, enlightenment rationalism, German idealism, the conservative reaction to the French and industrial revolutions, and many others'.[31] A sociology of sociologists, then, would suggest that theology may act as an independent variable in this context too.

This second approach as a whole goes hand in hand with the first. It would doubtless be possible to study the social determinants of theological positions in isolation. Yet it would be hard to justify such study from the sociological perspective if in fact theology can never act as an independent sociological variable. That is, if theology is without social significance, an analysis of its social determinants may command little attention.

This last approach is the one that will be explored in this book. I will argue at length that the theologian inevitably makes certain societal assumptions and that in doing so it is vital that he turn to the sociologist. Accordingly, the latter can perform an important function in discerning the social context which the theologian must take into consideration if he is to communicate at all.

This approach is different from the first in that it is not concerned with exposing the social determinants of particular theological positions. Rather it is concerned with the general social context within which the theological perspective operates. Nor is it specifically concerned with the possibility that this perspective may act as an independent variable within contemporary society.

It is clear that this approach is primarily oriented towards the needs of the theologian rather than those of the sociologist—though, hopefully, it will not be entirely irrelevant to the latter. It employs sociological evidence and explanations only in so far as these are relevant to theology and to the theological enterprise. By following this approach I hope to show that sociology is indeed of central importance to the theologian and that the latter ignores it at his peril.

However, it should be stressed at this stage that this book is basically concerned with methodology. I do not intend to offer any thoroughgoing substantive account of *the* social context of contemporary theology. Only an exhaustive inquiry would expose the full range of such a context. Instead, I intend solely to suggest the means by which one might establish an adequate understanding of this context.

Precisely because this study handles both theological and sociological material it raises fundamental methodological problems in both disciplines. The sociologist might suggest that this work is simply an exercise in 'religious sociology', whereas the theologian might argue that sociology is ill equipped to handle theological material. Accordingly, in the next chapter I will examine critically the traditional, and somewhat disparaging, distinction that is often made in sociology between 'religious sociology' and the 'sociology of religion'. It is a crucial methodological issue that cannot be ignored in a work such as this. This examination will lead naturally to the subsequent chapter on the role and status of 'explanation' in both theology and the sociology of religion.

Since the social context of theology is a relatively unexplored area these preliminary methodological considerations are vital. There is no universally accepted 'sociological method', just as there is none in theology. Consequently, it is important to make explicit the distinctions that I intend to use in subsequent chapters. However, the full force of these preliminary considerations will only become clear in the final chapter.

It will soon become apparent that this study is very different from that of the French 'religious sociologists'. Whereas they were concerned to apply sociological findings to the mission of the Church, I intend to apply sociology to the technical area of theology. Nevertheless, 'religious sociologists' such as Ferdinand Boulard were faced in part with similar problems. The latter described his work as follows:

> Religious sociology has a modest role in mission. It is an auxiliary science of pastoral policy, in the same way as psychology, pedagogy or medicine. It is at the service of pastoral theology, which directs the work of the Church towards 'the edification of the Body of Christ,' by making available a better understanding of human milieus and their influence upon the behaviour of the individuals who live in them. By so doing it indicates to responsible authority those sectors which are most menaced and the influences which cause the danger. It brings into the open, over and above the Christian history of individuals, the course of salvation in geographical regions and social milieus.[32]

Despite repeated criticism from both sociologists and theologians, Boulard maintained that this is a legitimate exercise. To the latter he suggested that 'religious sociology' has not 'undertaken the task of calculating the chances of Christianity in our world, as if we thought they depended only on immediate results'.[33] To the former he suggested that sociology can indeed be a pragmatic discipline. It is to this debate that I must turn next.

2

The Critique of Religious Sociology

'RELIGIOUS SOCIOLOGY' tends to be treated with disdain by both sociologists and theologians. Whereas the sociologist may regard it as a perversion of 'authentic' sociology, the theologian may see it as an intrusion of the 'secular' social scientist into matters that properly belong to a transcendental perspective. Despite its early and enthusiastic adoption in France, 'religious sociology' has come to be regarded with a good deal of suspicion.

The sociologist usually distinguishes between the 'sociology of religion' and 'religious sociology'. Sometimes a further distinction is made, 'Christian sociology', though it has little in common with what is normally understood to be sociology: it refers instead to a theological critique of the social order,[1] a task that may or may not require the assistanse of the academic sociologist. In the distinction between the 'sociology of religion' and 'religious sociology', it is only the first which is generally thought by the sociologist to belong to his particular perspective.

Sociological Objections to Religious Sociology

There are several reasons for the sociologist thinking it important to distinguish between 'religious sociology' and the 'sociology of religion', and for claiming that the former does not come within the province of academic sociology. Three reasons in particular might be isolated.

In the first place, it is generally argued that the sociologist of religion attempts to adopt a neutral stance in relation to the beliefs, practices and experiences that he is examining[2]. Essentially, he is not concerned with validity[3]: whether or not there really is a God, or whether or not Christ was the Son of God, are not issues that the sociologist as a sociologist can decide, or even matters with which he should be concerned. Nor can the Holy Spirit be given a place within the sociological perspec-

15

tive to act as an independent religious variable. Sociology must be strictly neutral on the issue of transcendence, since only in this way can religious-minded and non-religious-minded sociologists approach the sociology of religion on an equal basis.

In contrast, it is held that religious sociology is not strictly neutral in this sense. It demands a prior act of religious commitment from its adherents, or at least a prior act of commitment to furthering religious ideals or structures—whether in the form of the technical area of theology or in the shape of institutional Churches. So, it is pointed out that the pioneers of religious sociology were French Roman Catholics, whose basic aim was to further the work of the Catholic Church. The sociologist might argue that, however commendable this study might be in itself, it is not a part of sociology, and should be contained within the seminary rather than the university.

Secondly it is commonly argued that the sociology of religion and religious sociology are dependent on different traditions. Whereas the former is dependent on the sociological tradition, the latter relies on a theological one[4]. Certainly, those engaged in contemporary sociology of religion usually, though not always,[5] maintain that it belongs to the sociological tradition as a whole and can be used to test and illuminate sociological theories lying outside the sociology of religion. So, for example, the sociology of knowledge[6], the sociology of deviance[7], and organisational sociology[8] have all been related at times to the sociology of religion. In fact, the comparative neglect of the sociology of religion within both Britain and the States between the 1930s and the 1950s was only overcome by sociologists of religion acting in this way and justifying their study in relation to sociology as a whole.

Religious sociology, on the other hand, is usually thought by sociologists to have a theological, rather than sociological, dependency. As a discipline it is primarily answerable to the Church or to the theological perspective and not to sociology as a whole. It simply uses sociological techniques: it does not seriously test sociological theory. On this basis it could be maintained that, whereas the sociology of religion is a subdivision of sociology in general, religious sociology is essentially a parasitic discipline. Certainly the latter may at times produce data which are of interest to the sociologist—most sociologists of religion do refer at times to the work of Boulard[9] or Fichter[10]—but its primary reference lies outside sociology.

Finally, it could be argued that the sociology of religion, like any other legitimate academic discipline, pursues knowledge for its own sake, whereas religious sociology has a far more pragmatic orientation. The sociologist is not concerned about the 'usefulness' of his enterprise, and would consider such a category irrelevant to his discipline. In studying religion he is not ideologically motivated: he is not interested in how far his analysis of religion will be useful either to the religious or the non-religious. Instead, he finds religion an interesting phenomenon in its own right, which can be studied in the same spirit in which one might study Homeric Greek. The academic study of anything is self-justifying—as long as there are people who wish to study it, it should be studied.

The position of the sociologist in relation to religious sociology, then, seems clear. The sociology of religion and religious sociology are entirely separate disciplines, despite their common use of the word 'sociology'. Further, the academic sociologist rightly regards religious sociology with caution because it is not neutral, it does not relate to sociological theory as a whole and it is not a self-contained and detached discipline. Instead it is religiously committed, theologically dependent and pragmatically oriented in a way that the sociology of religion is not.

Theological Objections to Religious Sociology

If religious sociology tends to be dismissed by sociologists, it fares little better in the hands of theologians. Despite an apparently growing use of sociological techniques by the Churches in the West, there is also evidence of considerable resistance to these techniques.

The reaction to Leslie Paul's report *The Deployment and Payment of the Clergy* in 1964 well illustrates this resistance. Paul, although a theologian himself, deliberately adopted the techniques of the social scientist in the hope that 'the rejection of emotive terms will enable us to keep a certain coolness and objectivity in assessing the evidence'.[11] Whatever the specific sociological deficiencies of the report[12], it undoubtedly revealed discrepancies both in deployment and payment within the

17

Church of England at the time. Writing six years later, however, Paul pointed out that, due to the decline in ordinands, the situation had actually deteriorated in the Church of England. Somewhat bitterly, he wrote:

> Briefly the present ministry of the Church of England is an aging group, a declining group, a misused group and (in urban areas) an overworked group. The Church has rejected the rationalising proposals of my report and the severer Fenton Morley Report. These would at least have led over a period to the most effective use of the existing ministry. *The Pastoral Measure* (1968) provides some way round problems of shortage and of mission needs if dioceses have the courage to use it—it does make provision for the complete re-organisation of areas in the light of missionary needs—but it is a slow and piecemeal means of reform. It looks, by the temper of Church Assembly, July 1970 (which rejected Fenton Morley and proposed yet another commission), as though the Church will wait in inertia for the shocks of erosion to shove it into action. But a Church aging in more senses than the historical may be impeded by hardening of the arteries when the time comes and may deeply regret the wasted decade of the sixties.[13]

Paul's obvious disillusionment was caused, not simply by the 'inertia' of the Church of England, but also by the fact that his report was rejected in part on *theological grounds*. So, for example, the Bishop of Pontefract, Eric Treacy, claimed that 'whilst not denying the need for clear heads and a recognition of facts in ordering the life of the Church, we must ever have in mind that the Spirt bloweth where it listeth, and that the Spirit can make nonsense of statistics and sociological surveys'.[14] Treacy suggested that the 'character' of the Church of England— 'a mixture of cunning, laziness, and peasant simplicity'—renders it 'absorbent and impregnable' and impervious to sociological techniques.[15]

One of the central objections of the theologian to sociology, perhaps, is that it tends to ignore the transcendent. This objection can be expressed at both an institutional and an individual level.

At the institutional level, it may be felt that the sociologist systematically excludes the possibility that the Holy Spirit may in any way guide or influence the Church. That is, the Holy Spirit is never treated as an independent religious variable. Precisely because the sociological method adopts a thoroughly finite system of causality, it excludes any system of transcedent causality. Such a method may be adequate for the sociologist of religion, but it is likely to be most inadequate for the theologian, since it ignores the one element that he considers to be significant about the Church.[16]

At the individual level, the theologian may well feel uneasy about attempts by sociologists to quantify religiosity. I shall be returning to such attempts in Chapter 7, but for the moment it is sufficient to note that the theologians may believe that they are fundamentally mistaken. For the theologian the concept of 'faith', which is essentially unquantifiable, may be more apposite than that of 'religiosity'—since the concept of 'faith' takes into account the transcedent role of grace within the individual believer. No sociological account of individual religiosity— whether it is based on the data from questionnaire-surveys or on generalized statistics of religious practice—will ever be able to provide an account of individual faith. Certainly the 'religious maps' provided by Boulard[17] or John Gay[18]—based as they are on churchgoing statistics—will hardly give the theologian an adequate impression of the locality of individual faith in France or Britain.

The second major criticism that theologians may make of the use of sociology in the context of religion concerns the presumed tendency of the social sciences to 'explain away' religious phenomena. It seems apparent that some of the most distinguished pioneers of the social sciences—notably, Marx, Durkheim and Freud—were inclined to 'explain away' religion and religious phenomena—whether as 'a sop for the masses' in a situation of elitist stratification, as the product of man's 'sociability', or as a neurotic perpetuation of childhood fantasies. Further, it is known that all three men were inclined to be somewhat hostile towards 'orthodox' religion in the West.

The apparent 'neutrality' of contemporary sociologists of religion may not totally immunise them from this criticism, despite their claim that they are no longer concerned with the validity of religion. It is always possible to argue that the tendency of the pioneer sociologists to 'explain away' religious

19

phenomena remains implicit within the sociological perspective, The very fact that the sociologist seeks social determinants of all human behaviour commits him to the view that religion must be 'explained away'.

A part of this criticism remains even when it is admitted that it rests upon two fundamental errors. The first is that few of the pioneers of the social sciences really did attempt to 'explain away' religious phenomena *in toto*. Certainly they were concerned to provide explanations of the origins and function of religion, but both Durkheim and Freud claimed that this was not tantamount to 'explaining away' religion, whatever their own personal religious beliefs.

The second error follows from the first. The confusion of origins with validity is a fundamental philosophical mistake (the generic fallacy). To say that x is caused by y is to say nothing at all about the validity of x on logical grounds, no matter how disreputable y might be. Nevertheless, a point remains which can, perhaps, be best illustrated with an example I have used elsewhere.[19]

Suppose, for example, that John Allegro's extraordinary thesis about the origins of Christianity being linked with a psychodelic mushroom cult really were substantiated. How would this affect Christian belief? Logically, it need not, since the Christian could always claim that the origins of his beliefs do not affect their validity. So, it would be logically possible for the Christian to remain a Christian, claiming that God could have wrought salvation through a mushroom cult if he had so desired. However, there is something rather odd psychologically about this claim. It would seem more likely that many Christians would lose their confidence in the validity of Christianity, since they would find it psychologically difficult to remain adherents of such an extraordinary faith. Whilst admitting on logical grounds that God could have acted in this way, in practice they would be inclined to think otherwise. Clearly, then, the origins of beliefs are not altogether irrelevant to their validity—at least, for most people they are not.

The theologian's suspicion of the social scientist may well be justified precisely at this point. It is not necessary for the latter to be attempting to 'explain away' religion: it is enough that he seeks causal explanations whilst studying religious phenomena. The social scientist can give no guarantee to the theologian that these causal explanations will always prove harmonious with religious belief. Indeed, the accounts of the function of religion provided by Marx, Durkheim and Freud may well prove psychologically distressing for the Christian.

Both of these criticisms—based on a tendency to ignore the transcendent and to provide distressing causal explanations— are really overall criticisms of the social sciences in so far as they consider religious phenomena. A final criticism, however, might be suggested which is peculiarly applicable to religious sociology. It is based on the tendency of religious sociologists to move too quickly from sociological descriptions to theological prescriptions.[20] I shall return to this criticism in Chapter 4 when I consider Harvey Cox's *The Secular City*. This tendency is, however, a major weakness in socio-theological correlations. From both the theological and the sociological perspectives it is an error to assume a logical link between sociological analysis, explanations and even predictions, and the sort of prescriptive language the theologian legitimately employs.

Objections Reviewed

I have suggested, then, that six fundamental criticisms might be made of religious sociology—three from the sociologist and three from the theologian. The former might criticise the discipline because it is religiously committed, theologically dependent and pragmatically oriented in a way that the sociology of religion is not. The latter might criticise it because it tends to ignore the transcendent, to provide distressing causal explanations and to move too easily from sociological descriptions to theological prescriptions. An examination of these criticisms should help to clarify some of the methodological distinctions that I am employing in this study.

The sociological argument based on 'neutrality' is becoming increasingly difficult to maintain with conviction. Even a casual examination of the spread of interests amongst sociologists is sufficient to confirm the impression that sociology is seldom value-free. Some notable theorists, both in sociology in general,[21] and in the sociology of religion in particular,[22] have argued that the values and ideologies of sociologists do exert an influence upon their work. If this were not the case, the lack of interest

21

amongst sociologists in religious phenomena between the 1920s
and 1950s would be hard to explain. Inevitably, the particular
interests of sociologists are, at least partially, determined by
the contemporary interests of the academic community as a
whole. So at a time following the logical positivists, when
academic interest in religion was at a fairly low level both in
Britain and in the States, the comparative neglect of religious
phenomena by sociologists is understandable—understandable,
certainly, but incredible if sociology is to be regarded as value-
free.

It is possible that the notion that sociology is in some sense
'neutral' springs from an out-dated system of induction. Once
it was commonly thought that the scientist employed an inductive method of approaching reality. That is, he dispassion-
ately observed phenomena until they suggested laws to him,
which he could then frame into theories, and which in turn
he could test empirically. On the assumption that sociology is a
science it appears that some sociologists did in fact view their
work in this way.[23] Today, however, there generally appears
to be a greater humility amongst scientists, and a readiness to
admit that the scientist's own imagination—creative imagination—plays an important role in the formation of scientific
theories. The scientist does not approach his work in a dis-
passionate and value-free way: instead he approaches it
creatively.[24]

Amongst some contemporary social theorists, too, there is a
greater readiness to admit that sociological theory is based not
on a system of induction, but on the creative use of models.[25]
Consequently, it becomes increasingly difficult to maintain that
the sociology of religion is indeed a 'neutral' or value-free enterprise and to criticise religious sociology for not being so. Instead
a genuinely scientific methodology would seem to demand the
admission that we all have value-biases, but that we should
make these explicit in so far as this is possible, rather than retain
them implicitly in a seemingly value-free theory.

Of course, this argument can be pressed too far. It is unnecessary to claim that personal values and religious orientations
dominate all scientific examinations of religious phenomena.
Ninian Smart suggests two reasons for supposing that this may
not be the case:

22

First, there are degrees of bias: some omnipresent bias does not legitimate universal great bias; and second, more importantly, does a scholar's position *legitimately* influence his conclusions in this sphere? In the latter case there has to be some logical or intrinsic connection between his beliefs and his role as explorer of religion. Otherwise, the lament that men are liable to weaknesses and distortions which impede their goals is an old one; we know that men are imperfect, but they can become *better* at doing things if they set their hearts on it. (One thing they could do is to leave the study of religion to those who are least inclined to bias!) The objection, then, can only hold if there is a logical connection between the scholar's position and the kind of conclusion he ought to arrive at.[26]

Boulard has always maintained that his account of religious sociology does have scientific status.[27] On Smart's suggestion, the way to test this claim would be to see whether or not his conclusions can be logically derived from his initial religiously-oriented premises. It is insufficient simply to point out that he is a French Roman Catholic priest working for the Church.

If religious sociology cannot automatically be dismissed on the basis that it is value-oriented, it is difficult to see why it should be labelled as 'theologically dependent'. In so far as religious sociologists really do think of themselves as sociologists, and not simply as theologians using a certain amount of sociological techniques, they should theoretically be able to relate their findings to sociology as a whole. Granted they should initially make their value-orientation explicit, they should then be able to contribute to the sociological enterprise on an equal footing with other sociologists.

Perhaps it is the third criticism—based on the notion that the sociology of religion pursues knowledge for its own sake, whereas religious sociology is a pragmatic discipline related to the needs of theology and the Church—that causes the greatest discontent amongst sociologists. This appears to be a real distinction between the two disciplines which proponents of each might accept.

However, it is possible that the sociology of religion is rather unusual as a sociological discipline in so far as it does attempt to avoid a pragmatic basis. In many ways the sociological enterprise as a whole is thoroughly based in pragmatism. Few object to the use of sociological theory in the fields of industry, education, deviance or race relations. In all these areas sociology is used at times for pragmatic ends: a need is felt in some way to improve the status quo and the sociologist is unashamedly used to help with this task. Of course, it would be quite possible for the sociologist to be engaged in any of these four areas simply on the basis of pursuing 'knowledge for its own sake'. Yet, in practice, both the research grants made available by people engaged in these areas and the value-orientations of sociologists themselves contradict this possibility. Sociological analysis *is* used extensively on a purely pragmatic basis.

If this is the case in other areas of sociology, it is difficult to see why it should not be so in the specific area of the sociology of religion. Boulard, too, is aware of this criticism:

> It hardly seems worth replying at length to those who fear that a scientific piece of work is falsified by the intention to make pastoral or missionary use of its results. Has the concern to save human lives ever compromised the scientific quality of medical research? It must, of course, be stressed that only rigorous impartial observation of the facts can produce legitimate conclusions for formulating policy.[28]

Boulard's point remains despite his optimism about 'impartial observation' and 'the facts'.

Once it is admitted that the sociology of religion is not value-free and that religious sociology is not necessarily theologically dependent, this final criticism becomes increasingly difficult to maintain. In other areas of sociology it is not usual to make a sharp distinction between sociologists who pursue 'knowledge for its own sake' and those who have some pragmatic orientation. Provided that both types of sociologist act within the accepted framework of the sociological perspective, their contributions tend to be considered together. Further, if the distinction between the sociology of religion and religious sociology is to be maintained simply on the basis that the first is concerned with religion 'for its own sake', whereas the second is pragmatically oriented, it is difficult to see that it will hold up in practice. At what point does religious sociology become sociology of religion, and vice versa?

From the sociological perspective alone it seems that the

traditional distinction between religious sociology and the sociology of religion should be abandoned even if it was useful in the past. It cannot be maintained successfully on the basis of either the supposed value-orientation or the alleged theological dependency of religious sociology. In addition, there seems little point in rigorously distinguishing between those who are concerned about religious phenomena 'for their own sake' and those who are not—even if such a rigorous distinction could be maintained in practice. Doubtless some sociologists will be prepared to work pragmatically for theology or for the Church, whereas others will not. But this preparedness will not serve to differentiate them as either religious sociologists or sociologists of religion.

Finally, there is a non-sociological reason for wishing to abandon the traditional title 'religious sociology'. As a title it is peculiarly unfortunate, since it appears to imply that there are two types of sociology—the one 'religious' and the other presumably 'non-religious'. Doubtless, this implication was not originally intended, but it does appear to be conveyed by the title. By abandoning it this embarrassment is removed.

The objections of the theologian to the use of sociology in the context of theology, however, remain—particularly the claims that the sociologist tends to ignore the transcendent and to provide distressing causal explanations. These will be the subject of the next chapter.

3

Explanation in Sociology and Theology

THE ROLE and status of 'explanation' in both the sociology of religion and theology are crucial to most theological criticisms of the use of sociology in the context of theology. It is possible, in fact, that many of these criticisms are based on inadequate understandings of sociological 'explanations', particularly as they apply to religious phenomena.

In the previous chapter I suggested three main theological objections to the use of sociology; such use tends to ignore the transcendent, to provide distressing causal explanations and to move too easily from sociological descriptions to theological descriptions. However, I will defer the last of these objections to the next chapter. It is clear, though, that those who wish to employ sociology in the context of theology should at least be aware of the difference between analysis, explanation and prediction, on the one hand, and prescription, on the other.

The theologian who is prepared to be open to the work of the sociologist can, of course, be given no guarantee that he will not at times be confronted with distressing causal explanations. So, for example, in the first chapter I suggested a number of ways in which theology may act as an independent variable within society. However, neither Weber's nor Glock and Stark's examples of this action may prove particularly congenial to the theologian. He may or may not regard it as welcome news that theology might have contributed to the rise of both capitalism and anti-Semitism in the West.

Possibly this is a risk that the theologian must take. It is certainly a risk that he has taken in other fields with considerable benefit. The results, for example, of both historical and philosophical criticism, even within theological faculties, have at times proved extremely distressing to theologians. Nevertheless, the latter do not usually suggest that these enterprises should on that account be ignored. On balance it might appear that the critical perspectives that both philosophical and historical analysis have contributed to theology have proved more beneficial than harmful. A similar case might be advanced for the use of sociology within the context of theology.

This solution, however, may only obscure the central objection of the theologian to sociology. The objection may not be simply that sociology offers distressing causal explanations, but that its basic methodology is fundamentally opposed to the theological perspective. Framed in this way, the objection comes close to the initial criticism—i.e. that sociology tends to ignore the transcendent. It is precisely at this point that the role and status of 'explanation' within both sociology and theology become crucial. If 'explanation' within the sociology of religion is to be interpreted in an imperialist and positivist fashion its relevance to the theological perspective becomes doubtful. At best theology must simply ignore sociology: at worst it must be rendered redundant by it.

The sociology of religion becomes imperialist when it claims to be *the* way of interpreting religious phenomena. Such a claim would, of course, affect the psychologist, anthropologist and philosopher, as much as the theologian. It becomes positivist when it claims that a behavioural interpretation of the social determinants of religious phenomena expresses the 'true' nature of these phenomena. This claim, if substantiated, would, of course, be as damaging to contemporary theology as the philosophical logical positivism of the Vienna Circle was to theology in the previous generation. If such imperialism and positivism are indeed implicit in sociological method, the prospects of any socio-theological correlation would be extremely remote.

The Limits of Sociological Explanation

A sophisticated form of this argument appears in John Bowker's examination of sociological, psychological and anthropological explanations of the sense of God. He maintains that all these forms of explanation, as they are usually expounded, are too restrictive. In the conclusion to his study he claims:

What has emerged quite separately in each of the various disciplines surveyed is an entirely new concern with the differen-

27

tiating consequences of the responsive objects of encounter. It is this which represents so important a revolution in recent years, because it implies a reversal of the nineteenth century ambition. It now becomes clear that we are not studying massive mechanisms of social process, or of individuation, alone, in which it is virtually irrelevant what objects are or are not encountered—as though the mechanism will in any case run on. It is the contributory effect of the actual objects of encounter which is returning into the analysis of behaviour in all these different disciplines.[1]

The effects of this claim in the specific context of the sense of God are radical. Bowker argues, in fact, that 'far from the disciplines we have been surveying dissolving the possible reality of reference in the term "God", they actually seem to demand a return to that possibility if sense is to be made of their own evidence'.[2]

Bowker maintains that he is not attempting to produce an argument for the existence of God—in no sense is his claim an implicit ontological argument for divine existence. However, he is determined to show from *within* the various disciplines that the possibility of the existence of God cannot be excluded, and may actually be demanded by the limitations of psychological, sociological and anthropological explanations of the sense of God. This is a discrete claim that he offers, but nevertheless an important and potentially radical one. Further, I suspect, it is a claim that few social scientists (whether they are themselves 'religious' or not) would be happy to support.

Bowker is not making the sort of crude theological objection which was noted in the previous chapter, whereby the social sciences are thought to 'explain away' religious phenomena. He is usually aware that, even if the social scientist could provide an adequate social explanation of the sense of God, this would still tell us very little about the reality of its reference. Like most Christians, he is dissatisfied with Freud's account, for example, of the origins of religion, but in general he argues against it on internal, rather than external, grounds. So, he claims that 'the basic defect of Freud's theory of religion is not that it cannot possibly be right, but that it cannot possibly be wrong: all evidence that superficially appears to contradict the theory is converted to become evidence *for* the theory'.[3] He does not claim from outside, so to speak, that Freud's theory is inadequate simply because it tends to conflate projection with invalidity.

Bowker's claim is that Freud and others did not take seriously the possibility that God could act as an independent variable within society. For him, an adequate analytical explanation of the sense of God—whether from the psychological, sociological or anthropological perspective—would have to take seriously the proposition that the origins of the sense of God are to be found, to some degree at least, in the relation of God himself to mankind.

The weakness of Bowker's claim becomes most apparent in his critical interpretation of Berger. He argues that the latter was originally too controlled 'by sociological orthodoxy' in his account of the social construction of religion and societal plausibility structures. He was too determined to interpret 'the social' solely in terms of 'the social':

> In *The Social Reality of Religion*, Berger completely missed this point. He got diverted into sociological orthodoxy—which in itself is not surprising, since sociologists, like all others, have to earn their way in the world, and are thus deeply constrained by norms and conventions of expectation in sociological community. Thus Berger, instead of exploring the possibility that there might be a sufficiency of reality in existence in the external universe for there to be a groundwork of perception on which interpretation can be constructed, suggested that the more important reality is the one which individuals confer on the external universe: individuals 'pour out meaning' into it, on the basis of the language and concepts which they have culturally acquired.[4]

In *A Rumour of Angels*, Bowker argues, Berger changed his mind, and was now prepared to examine 'signals of transcendence' contained within the universe. In the original book Berger stated baldy that 'religion is the human enterprise by which a sacred cosmos is established',[5] and claimed in effect that 'God is an artefact' and 'an end-product of socialisation',[6] but now he took seriously the possibility that the sacred cosmos' object could exercise an influence upon the human enterprise.

In fact, this is a misreading of Berger. The latter makes it quite plain in a foot-note to his claim that 'religion is the human enterprise by which a sacred cosmos is established', that he is well aware of the limitations of this sociological definition of religion:

> Religion is defined here as a human enterprise because this is how it manifests itself as an empirical phenomenon. Within this definition the question as to whether religion may also be something more than that remains bracketed, as, of course, it must be in any attempt at scientific understanding.[7]

In addition, Berger devotes a complete appendix to his book to 'sociological and theological perspectives'—arguing that 'no theological or, for that matter, anti-theological implications are to be sought anywhere in the argument—if anyone should believe such implications to be present *sub-rosa*, I can only assure him that he is mistaken'.[8] Essentially, the work is concerned with sociological theory, whereas *A Rumour of Angels* has a directly theological orientation. A careful comparison of the two works fails to substantiate Bowker's claim that Berger underwent a process of change between writing them.

The suggestion, however, that Berger is too strictly controlled by 'sociological orthodoxy' in *The Social Reality of Religion* must be taken more seriously. It is precisely at this point that the role and status of 'explanation' within sociology become crucial.

Berger suggests that there are three moments or steps in the process of socialisation (the process by which the individual interacts with society). He depicts these three steps as 'externalisation', 'objectivation', and 'internalisation'. Together these steps form the 'fundamental dialectic process of society':

> Externalization is the ongoing outpouring of human being into the world, both in the physical and mental activity of men. Objectivation is the attainment by the products of this activity (again both physical and mental) of a reality that confronts its original producers as a facticity external to and other than themselves. Internalisation is the reappropriation by men of this same reality, transforming it once again from structures of the objective world into structures of the subjective consciousness. It is through externalisation that society is a human product. It is through objectivation that society becomes a reality *sui generis*. It is through internalisation that man is a product of society.[9]

In the specific context of religious socialisation, these three steps are still apparent. Through externalisation the individual 'pours out meaning into reality'—he creates a 'sacred cosmos'. Through objectivation this 'sacred cosmos' assumes an objective identity—the 'sacred cosmos' of a particular society is presented to the child in that society as an objective reality. Through internalisation the individual himself is affected by the 'sacred cosmos' of the particular society in which he lives. Thus religion is indeed regarded by Berger in *The Social Reality of Religion* as a thoroughly human enterprise. It is created by society, it is then treated as an objective reality by that society and in turn it has an independent influence upon society—and should not be understood in strictly chronological terms.[10]

Again, Bowker objects that this account of religious socialisation does not take seriously the possibility of the reality of the reference in religious language. The latter, like all language, is regarded simply as a human product, an invention of society, and not as referring to objective reality. Further, at no point does he consider the possibility that the object of religious language—i.e. 'God' for Christians—can act as an independent variable in religious socialisation. Bowker, however, misses a vital element in Berger's methodology.

Methodological Atheism

Berger is well aware that he has excluded the transcendent from his sociological account of religious phenomena. He argues, however, that this exclusion is thoroughly necessary:

> In all its manifestations, religion constitutes an immense projection of human meanings into the empty vastness of the universe—a projection, to be sure, which comes back as an alien reality to haunt its producers. Needless to say, it is impossible within the frame of reference of scientific theorising to make any affirmations, positive *or* negative, about the ultimate ontological status of this alleged reality. Within this frame of reference, the religious projections can be dealt with only as such, as products of human activity and human consciousness, and rigorous brackets have to be placed around the question as to whether these projections may not *also* be something else than that (or, more accurately, *refer to* something else than the human world in which they empirically originate). In other words, every

31

inquiry into religious matters that limits itself to the empirically available must necessarily be based on a *'methodological atheism'*.[11]

Berger's concept of methodological atheism, then, *is* essentially a methodological, and not an ontological, stance. As a sociologist he believes that he has quite deliberately to exclude any reference to transcendent causality—whatever his personal religious beliefs. His whole concept of 'signals of transcendence' lies firmly outside his work as a sociologist of religion, since as a sociologist he is methodologically committed to viewing reality in exclusively empirical terms.

This 'methodological atheism' is different altogether from the sort of imperialist, positivist sociology noted earlier. Doubtless, the latter form of sociology still exists, just as it still exists in psychology.[12] John Rex, however, argues that such sociology tends to ignore Hume and suppose that causality is logically based. For him, 'the continued prevalence of purely causal enquiries in sociology is merely an indication of the extreme immaturity of the discipline, and we should expect that, as more adequate theories are developed, such enquiries will become part of a larger and more systematic plan of enquiry'.[13] Berger, however, is no positivist—nor could he be, unless his methodology were transformed into an ontology.

Ninian Smart, though, is not satisfied with Berger's 'methodological atheism'. He suspects that it is imperialist:

> He of course distinguishes this methodological atheism from atheism *tout court*. But one needs to ask what it is in the way of explanations that is excluded by methodological atheism. And further, is it merely a device for operating within 'scientific' sociology? If this be so, then is it assumed that a total account of explanation of religion can be given from a sociological point-of-view? The last is a very bold assumption, but less extravagant perhaps when one realises that sociological theory tends to subsume other spheres of human enquiry such as psychology within its embrace.[14]

Smart's three questions can be answered surprisingly simply. Berger makes it quite clear that his 'methodological atheism' is intended to exlude anything that is not 'empirically available'. He argues that the sociologist as a sociologist must concentrate solely upon the empirical. Consequently, Bowker's plea for a return *within* sociology to 'the possible reality of reference in the term "God"' is certainly excluded. Secondly, it is also clear that Berger proposes 'methodological atheism' precisely for operating within '"scientific" sociology': the latter, after all, is his speciality. And finally, there is no reason to believe that Berger ever imagined that 'a total account of explanation of religion can be given from a sociological point-of-view'. On the contrary, even within his description of 'methodological atheism' he leaves open the question of the ultimate reference of religious phenomena. If one also takes into account his more specifically theological writings, then it is abundantly clear that he is no sociological imperialist.

Only Smart's final point suggests a certain ambiguity within Berger's stated methodology. Like most sociologists, Berger seldom refers to psychological explanations of religious phenomena, yet these are not specifically excluded by his notion of methodological atheism. Psychological explanations plainly work with the 'empirically available', and, in theory at least, ought to form part of the perspective that Berger is proposing. Even the relative poverty of academic research into religious phenomena from the psychological perspective, does not in principle explain Berger's comparative neglect of the research that is available. It is possible, then, that the description of his methodology as 'methodological atheism' only partially depicts the methodology he is proposing.

A second, and less important, criticism might also be suggested. The term 'atheism' may be unfortunate, since it introduces too many extraneous connotations. Certainly it has prompted, *inter alia*, one sociologist to write:

> Berger is determined to surpass, if anything, the sceptics in their scepticism, and to show how cynically and debunkingly sociological a believing sociologist can be, before—just at the very last moment when all seems 'lost'—thrillingly producing an ace from his sleeve and coming out with a starkly absolute confession of faith.[15]

Certainly this is a caricature of Berger's position, but then the very notion of 'methodological *atheism*' may render him susceptible to such caricature.

Robert Towler's objections to 'methodological atheism', however, are far more severe. He argues, perhaps unfairly, that it is 'a fail-safe device which protects the sceptical researcher from taking the beliefs of others too seriously, and which protects also the religiously or ideologically committed researcher from allowing his own beliefs to pollute his research'.[16] In contrast, Towler believes that 'the sociologist's task, difficult and uncomfortable though it may be, is to take seriously the beliefs of those whom he studies and to seek to enter into the mentality which they bring to their ritual and to their everyday lives, even if in so doing he runs the risk of "going native"'.[17] His position is thus closer to Bellah's 'symbolic realism' than Berger's 'methodological atheism'.

Symbolic Realism

In proposing his research stance of 'symbolic realism', Robert Bellah deliberately intends to counter sociological literalists and reductionists. He believes that the position of 'symbolic realism' represents a fundamental break-through for those concerned with the study of religious phenomena—and, in particular, for the sociologist of religion.

Bellah identifies two kinds of sociological reductionism. In the first place there is 'consequential reductionism', which is concerned exclusively with 'the explanation of religion in terms of its functional consequences'.[18] This type of reductionism, or positivism, he sees as typical of those eighteenth-century 'secular intellectuals' who opposed the 'historical realism' of contemporary theologians. For 'consequential reductionists' the claims of Christianity were basically fraudulent. During the nineteenth century, however, Bellah argues that 'symbolic reductionism' arose. This type of reductionism no longer regarded religion as fraudulent: rather it was concerned with 'the search for the kernel of truth hidden in the falsity of religion'.[19] Thus, both Durkheim and Freud 'developed comprehensive formulas for the translation of religious symbols into their real meanings';[20] the latter in terms of the Oedipus complex and the former in terms of society itself.

Bellah argues, however, that Freud, Durkheim and Weber all encountered difficulties in their interpretations. Freud was confronted with the 'unconscious', Durkheim with the concept

34

of 'collective effervescence' and Weber with that of 'charisma'. In all three instances the pioneer social scientists were faced with irreducible, non-literal concepts. For Bellah this observation is crucial:

> What I am suggesting is that the fact that these three great non-believers, the most seminal minds in modern social science, each in his own way ran up against nonrational, noncognitive factors of central importance to the understanding of human action, but which did not yield readily to any available conceptual resources, is in itself a fact of great significance for religion in the twentieth century. Convinced of the invalidity of traditional religion, each rediscovered the power of the religious consciousness. What could perhaps be suggested on the basis of the work of these men is that when Western religion chose to make its stand purely on the ground of cognitive adequacy, it was forgetting the nature of the reality with which religion has to deal and the kind of symbols religion used.[21]

The new approach that arises from this observation is what Bellah terms 'symbolic realism'. Adopting this approach, he believes the sociology of religion is transformed. In his most modest description of this approach he suggests:

> Some social scientists have come to feel that there are profound depths in the religious symbols that we have scarcely begun to fathom and that we have much to learn from any exchange with other disciplines. While remaining committed to Enlightenment rationalism as the foundation of scientific work and accepting its canons with respect to our research, we nevertheless know that this is only one road to reality. It stands in tension with and under the judgement of other modes of consciousness. And finally we know that the great symbols that justify science itself rest on unprovable assumptions sustained at the deepest levels of our consciousness.[22]

From this account of 'symbolic realism' it would appear that Bellah is offering a number of straightforward methodological proposals. Firstly, he is suggesting that the sociologist of religion should take account of the 'profound depths' of the symbols he uses. Others too within a number of disciplines— psychology,[23] philosophy,[24] science[25] and theology[26]—have suggested that models or symbols should at times be viewed as irreducible and non-literal. Secondly, he is objecting to sociological imperialism, and maintaining instead that sociology is just 'one road to reality'. Thirdly, he does not intend to abandon the 'scientific' nature of sociology, even in its application to religious phenomena. Fourthly, he appears to have some implicit notion of the complementarity of methodologies, whereby sociology is regarded as a separate, but interacting, discipline. And fifthly, he admits that the symbols which are employed within scientific methodologies are themselves unprovable.

All five proposals are important and I shall freely employ them in the context of my final chapter. Together they help to present a more sophisticated picture of the sociological method than is sometimes offered.

However, Bellah's account of 'symbolic realism' does not conclude here. Only in part is it a methodology: it is also in part an ideology. This becomes plain from his celebrated claim that 'religion is true', or rather, less misleadingly, 'religion is a reality *sui generis*':

> When I say religion is a reality *sui generis* I am certainly not supporting the claims of the historical realist theologians, who are still working with a cognitive conception of religious belief that makes it parallel to objectivist scientific description. But if the theologian comes to his subject with the assumptions of symbolic realism, as many seem to be doing, then we are in a situation where for the first time in centuries theologian and secular intellectual can speak the same language. Their tasks are different but their conceptual framework is shared. What this means for the reintegration of our fragmented culture is almost beyond calculation.[27]

So attractive does he find the work of theologians such as Paul Tillich, that he continues that the sociologist must communicate 'the meaning and value of religion along with its analysis' to his students—thereby admitting that 'if this seems to confuse the role of theologian and scientist, of teaching religion and teaching about religion, then so be it'.[28]

It should be stressed, however, that Bellah is not proposing anything comparable to Bowker's plea for a return *within* sociology to 'the possible reality of reference in the term "God"'. He would probably identify Bowker's plea as 'historical realism'. For Bellah religious symbols 'tell us nothing at all about the universe except insofar as the universe is involved in human experience.'[29] His proposals, though, do face the very real possibility that the methods of 'symbolic realist' sociologists and 'symbolic realist' theologians may eventually become conflated.

It is precisely at this point that the weakness of Bellah's proposals for the sociology of religion becomes most apparent. Once they become an ideology they may be of considerable use to the theologian, but of distinctly less use to the sociologist. As I stressed in the previous chapter, it is vital that the sociology of religion should be viewed as a part of the sociological discipline as a whole. If it is too closely conflated with theology it may cease to be relevant to general sociological theory.

Even as a methodology 'symbolic realism' cannot be regarded as furnishing a complete account of the basis on which the sociologist of religion must operate. As an account it may be viewed as an extended plea for 'empathy' within the sociology of religion, and for a more sophisticated set of models. However, in the context of certain 'conversionist' Sects 'empathy' has been found to be a dangerous research method, since researchers adopting it were always misunderstood by Sect members unable to distinguish between 'empathy' and a desire for 'conversion'.[30]

An 'As If' Methodology

A more fruitful account of the basis on which the sociologist in general, and the sociologist of religion in particular, operates, might be found in an 'as if' methodology. Adopting such a methodology the sociologist would work 'as if' there were social determinants of all human interactions—believing as an individual, though, that there may not be. Like Berger's 'methodological atheism' such a stance would be methodological, not ontological, and thereby immune from charges of positivism, behaviourism or imperialism. Like Bellah's 'symbolic realism' it might recognise the need for irreducible, non-literal societal models, such as would be necessary, for example, to take into account the complex character of religious symbols and beliefs.

An 'as if' methodology would, I believe, avoid the weaknesses evident in the proposals of both Berger and Bellah. It offers a more generalised theory than Berger's 'methodological atheism': the latter leaves the impression that there is something peculiar

37

about the sociologist of religion, whereas the former allows for an overall theory of methodologies in general, whether or not they are concerned with specifically religious phenomena. Again, an 'as if' methodology deliberately seeks to avoid the sort of socio-theological conflation apparent in Bellah: sociology and theology are regarded as distinct, even if complementary disciplines.

Contemporary anthropology provides an interesting illustration of the use of an 'as if' methodology. At one stage behaviourism and functionalism appeared to be the dominant methodologies within social anthropology. Today, however, this domination would no longer appear to be so evident. The almost biological view of social morphology and structure, for example, that was once so popular, today is often questioned.[31] Edmund Leach, however, has argued that traditional techniques for studying social change should not be abandoned, even if their positivist framework is itself abandoned:

> In practical field work situations the anthropologist must always treat the material of observation *as if* it were a part of an overall system of equilibrium, otherwise description becomes impossible. All that I am asking is that the fictional nature of this equilibrium be frankly recognised.[32]

On this understanding of the sociological method, then, the sociologist, in so far as he remains a sociologist, is obliged to treat religious phenomena as if they were purely social phenomena—whatever his private views about the validity or falsity of religious truth-claims. He is not obliged to believe that religious phenomena *are* purely social phenomena: but he is obliged to take sociological theory sufficiently seriously not to exclude—either *a priori* or *a posteriori*—any particular religious phenomenon from his examination.

This understanding will also explain, perhaps, why sociology often appears imperialistic vis à vis other disciplines. So, Smart's claim that 'sociological theory tends to subsume other spheres of human enquiry such as psychology within its embrace' becomes explicable, since it is the job of the sociologist to examine human interaction as if it were entirely socially determined. This is a deliberate methodological stance, not an act of sociological chauvinism.

It is arguable, for instance, that Berger is wrong when he categorically states that 'hardly anyone, however far removed from sociological thinking, is likely to deny that language is a human product', and that 'there are no laws of nature that can be called upon to explain the development of, say, the English language'.[33] Contemporary supporters of Chomsky's transformational linguistic theory might wish to qualify such a claim, and it would be right that they should do so. However, it would also be right for Berger, qua sociologist, to examine human language as if it were solely a product of society, and nothing at all to do with innate brain structures. There is in fact a distinctly pre-Chomsky ring to Berger's claim, and he possibly is intending to make an 'is' statement. Nevertheless, it remains possible for him to make a similar statement employing an 'as if' sociological method.

The importance of the deliberate fiction involved in an 'as if' methodology has been known since Vaihinger. He claimed that 'the object of the world of ideas as a whole is not the portrayal of reality—this would be an utterly impossible task—but rather to provide us with an *instrument for finding our way about more easily in this world*'.[34] In terms of such an object the methodological fiction plays an important role. So, for example, contemporary science is presumably only possible if one adopts an 'as if' methodology. An individual scientist might well be convinced by Hume's attack on straightforward logical notions of 'causality', or by Popper's attack on 'verification' as opposed to 'falsification'. Nevertheless, he must still continue his work as if there was a logical relationship between cause and effect, and as if verification were indeed possible. He may be a humbler man than his positivist predecessors, but he is not ground to inactivity by his knowledge of Hume and Popper.

If the sociologist is committed to a methodology whereby he views human interaction as if there were always social determinants of it, the theologian will be clearly committed to some other methodology. In contrast to Bellah and Bowker, I would suggest that the theologian is committed to a radically different 'as if' methodology. He views the world as if there were transcendent determinants of it. It is he, not the social scientist, who must take seriously 'the possible reality of ference in the term "God"'.

It will become apparent in succeeding chapters that I consider that these two methodologies, different as they are, can at times be complementary. The final demonstration of this complementarity, however, must remain until the last chapter. For the moment, it is clear that an 'as if' methodology in both disciplines, if adopted, would make them immune to the sort of imperialism and positivism that has bedevilled socio-theological correlations in the past.

PART TWO

Theological Plausibility Structures

4

Theologians and Amateur Sociologists

AN ACCOUNT of the social context of theology presupposes both
that the sociological perspective is not necessarily in conflict
with the theological perspective, as I argued in the previous
chapter, and that it is actually relevant to it. Naturally, the latter
is not without critics, though in the next chapter I will argue at
length that it is a correct presupposition. More specifically, I will
argue that theologians must take note of the social context
within which they operate, because otherwise they will cease to
be effective theologians.

In this chapter, however, I will examine just two contemporary
theologians—Harvey Cox and John Robinson—who do in fact
take contemporary society seriously, and who both attempt to
provide an analysis of the social context within which they work.
These two theologians have been chosen for didactic, rather
than representative, purposes. Clearly they are both proponents
of a fairly radical theology within Britain and the States and
could not be regarded as typical of all shades of theological
opinion. My purpose, though, in using them is primarily methodological: hopefully, they will serve to uncover some of the pit-
falls that confront those attempting socio-theological correlations.
It will emerge that I believe a far more sophisticated form of
correlation is necessary than is at present evident within
theology.

The Secular City

Much of the initial criticism of Harvey Cox's highly successful
The Secular City centred upon his distinction between the
'secular' and the 'religious'.[1] Partially, he may have been the
victim of later theological developments, since increasingly in the
latter part of the 1960s the focus of theological debate was on the
so-called 'death of God' theologians. Somewhat unfairly, perhaps,
they were often seen as identical to theologians such as Cox

and Robinson, and the latter themselves tended to be classified as 'atheists', or, at least, as 'non-theists'. For Cox, in particular with his dependence on neo-orthodox theology, such labelling was inappropriate. 'Secular' for him was not at all identical with 'non-theistic'. Rather his criticism, both in *The Secular City* and elsewhere,[2] was of the categories of 'religion' and the 'religious'.

Today there appear to be few defenders of this once popular distinction between 'religion' and 'Christianity'. Even amongst Protestant theologians not all are prepared to dismiss specifically 'religious' phenomena as irrelevant to the Gospel.[3] A distinction that was once popular now appears to be untenable, and as a result *The Secular City* seems somewhat outmoded.

Nevertheless, there is at least one feature of the work which has continued to be influential, notably Cox's analysis of, and theological reaction to, the phenomenon of urbanisation. The concept of 'anonymity' played an important role within this analysis and reaction, and has proved to be one of the more stimulating features of the study. Possibly it is just here that Cox made his most interesting contribution, and it is certainly here that his socio-theological correlation becomes most evident.

By concentrating upon Cox's concept of 'anonymity' within *The Secular City*, I am not, of course, attempting an exhaustive critique of the work. That has been attempted many times before, and would in any case be irrelevant to the aims of this chapter. Rather, the purpose of examining this particular concept in this particular work is simply to observe how one theologian uses sociological data.

Although Cox was naturally not the first writer to claim that contemporary cities tend to be 'anonymous' and 'impersonal', he was one of the first theologians to applaud this aspect of cities. The suggestion that contemporary cities do possess these characteristics usually implies a negative criticism, since in this context 'anonymous' is often regarded as synonymous with 'soul-less' and 'dehumanised' (whatever such terms might mean).

Cox, then, starts with the assumption that cities are indeed characterised by 'anonymity':

> Every college sophomore knows that modern man is a face-less cipher. The stock in trade of too many humanities courses and

religious-emphasis weeks is the featureless 'mass man', reduced to a number of a series of holes in an IBM card, wandering through T.S. Eliot's 'waste land' starved for a name. 'Loss of identity' and 'disappearance of selfhood' have come to play an ever larger role in the popular pastime of flagellating urban culture[4]

He disagrees, however, with contemporary criticisms of this 'anonymity', and particularly with critics of urbanisation:

A writer who becomes *essentially* anti-urban forfeits his claim to greatness, for what is often left unsaid by the morbid critics of anonymity is, first, that without it life in a modern city would not be human, and second, that anonymity represents for many people a liberating even more than a threatening phenomenon. It serves for a large number of people as the possibility of freedom in contrast to the bondage of the law and convention. The anonymity of city living helps to preserve the privacy essential to human life. Furthermore, anonymity can be understood theologically as Gospel versus Law.[5]

The last sentence in this quotation is crucial. Cox is not simply claiming that urban 'anonymity' can be justified on purely humanitarian grounds, but that it is thoroughly Biblical. This becomes more apparent in the following passage:

How can urban anonymity be understood theologically? Here the traditional distinction between Law and Gospel comes to mind. In using these terms we refer not to religious rules or to fiery preaching, but to the tension between bondage to the past and freedom for the future. In this sense Law means anything that binds us uncritically to inherited conventions, and Gospel is that which frees us to decide for ourselves.[6]

There are, then, three parts to Cox's analysis of urban 'anonymity':

1. Sociological analysis—concluding that anonymity is characteristic of contemporary cities.
2. Humanitarian analysis—concluding that urban anonymity has beneficial features for mankind.
3. Theological analysis—concluding that urban anonymity is an expression of Gospel rather than Law.

Despite the overall appeal of this sociological-humanitarian-theological correlation, each of its parts must face serious criticisms.

1. *Sociological analysis*: Urban sociologists today are by no means all convinced that 'anonymity' *is* a characteristic of cities. One of the strongest critics of this notion is R.E. Pahl, who argues that 'the qualitative effects of quantitative changes are hard to assess and are not helpfully described by such terms as "urbanisation" which are almost impossible to define precisely'.[7] Pahl points out that 'individual autonomy' is a feature of the middle-classes, rather than the working-classes within cities: the latter are better characterised by 'values of us/them solidarity'. Further, he criticises monochrome treatments of 'urbanisation', showing instead that cities differ vastly. So, in one city a Coxian pattern of 'urbanisation' might be found, whereas in another an essentially rural culture might still be present amongst the working-classes. Even the much-discussed 'nuclear family' is by no means a feature of all cities. Pahl argues that at the beginning of the industrial revolution poverty and limited housing forced many working-class families to live together in extended families, and that present patterns of nuclear-family living may correspond fairly closely to pre-industrial, rural patterns of family life.

So, it is by no means clear that the first step in Cox's argument is accurate. His whole thesis depends on this step, since his theological interpretation is directly dependent on his sociological analysis. If it is the case that 'anonymity' is an ambiguous characteristic of contemporary cities, then the rest of his argument collapses.

2. *Humanitarian analysis*: It is significant, perhaps, that Cox's later writings are more reticent about the merits of contemporary cities. *The Feast of Fools*, for example, is less concerned with the merits of contemporary culture and more with its deficiencies. Cox maintains that the features of feasting and celebration are largely absent from culture today.

Just at this point in his writing, Cox comes closer to the position of a theologian like David Harned. For the latter, it is not so much the 'anonymity' of contemporary culture which he believes to be important, but the 'self-seriousness' of modern man.[8] In his criticisms of this 'self-seriousness' Harned re-

46

peatedly returns, not to the concepts of feasting and celebration, but to Johan Huizinga's notion of 'play', which he describes as a basic 'instinct' of man:

> In its pure form, play is, first of all, voluntary, an act of freedom. Since there is no utilitarian motivation for it, play can always be deferred. We never need to do it, except 'to the extent that the enjoyment of it makes it a need'. Secondly, there is always an element of conflict or tension involved in it, a striving either to determine some issue or to win some victory. It can be a contest for something or a representation of something. And sometimes it is both, as when children play at war. Thirdly, play calls us away from ordinary life into a realm with rules all its own and definite boundaries in time and space.[9]

Unlike that of Cox, this analysis makes no special claims for 'contemporary man', either meritorious or not, but merely attempts to analyse man as he is, finding him too 'self-serious' and lacking in 'play', or, more accurately, lacking in an acknowledgement of man as 'player'. Perhaps Harned himself lays too much stress on this model of man as 'player' in his writings— doubtless man needs other models too to depict him—but this is merely a question of emphasis, not of sociological accuracy.

Further, there *is* a demonic side to 'anonymity', which Cox ignores in his attempt to stress its positive humanitarian aspects. John Ferguson, for example, asks:

> But is the anonymity of urban life liberation? Plenty of people flock to the cities as a form of escape. But escape from what? Sometimes from themselves, from personal responsibility. Sometimes from a limited tribal society which they have found a shackle on their self-fulfilment; these last go to the city with the purpose of finding their true selves. Do they succeed?[10]

Ferguson clearly thinks that they do not. Instead he believes that there is an element within every encounter with others which is properly 'personal', and denies the sheer 'impersonality' of Cox's aspirations for society.

Finally, an anonymous environment, if indeed it exists, may be desirable only for those who are strong or well enough to choose freedom.[11] Such an environment is not nearly so desirable

47

for those who are hungry, poor, old or lonely—and all cities inevitably contain such people.

3. *Theological analysis*: Cox's theological analysis, too, may be criticised. Certainly his interpretation of the distinction between Law and Gospel as 'the tension between bondage to the past and freedom for the future'[12] gained few supporters. In isolation this sentence could come from Paul van Buren,[13] since, superficially at least, it appears to be a thoroughly non-transcendent theological interpretation of this tension. Whether or not this is actually the case, it is his theological methodology which is of peculiar interest in the present context.

It has already been seen that Cox's theological interpretation or urban anonymity is dependent on his sociological conclusions. He begins with the sociologist, moves to the humanitarian, and finally finds that this agrees with the Biblical evidence. A similar methodology is evident in Peter Rudge's analysis of the Church in terms of the sociological theory of organisations.[14] Of course, it is possible that sociology and theology may correspond so conveniently at times, but it is by no means clear that they always should or will. Both Cox and Rudge, in very different ways, are in danger of jumping straight from the 'is' to the 'ought'. Sociological descriptions and theological prescriptions become thoroughly confused.

This point is quite crucial. *The Secular City* was important precisely because it attempted a socio-theological correlation, but it committed too many blunders in the process. It is essential that an adequate correlation should distinguish carefully between analysis, explanation and prediction, on the one hand, and prescription, on the other—that is, between the 'is' and the 'ought'. If Cox had been better aware of this distinction in the material he was handling, he might have been more prepared to admit the obvious demonic aspects of 'anonymity'. The failure of the work at this point suggests that future correlations must be considerably more sophisticated.

This methodological problem is, perhaps, the major difficulty involved in *Ths Secular City*. However, the initial difficulty for the sociologist must be constituted by the accuracy of Cox's sociological analysis. Before a sophisticated socio-theological correlation can be attempted it is obviously essential that the sociological analysis adopted should be accurate. It is plainly fatuous to explore the social context of theology on the basis of faulty sociological data, yet this does seem to be the situation in *The Secular City.*

Cox is not unique in his approach. It is surprising, perhaps, how often contemporary theologians make suggestions about what 'modern man' thinks or does, without any reference to the work of sociologists. Yet it is quite clear that the theologian who is concerned to specify what 'modern man' thinks or does is *himself* acting as a sociologist—he is attempting to provide an analysis of society. In an age when academic sociology did not exist, it might have been permissible to provide such analysis, but at a time when this is no longer the case it must appear as somewhat strange.

The Human Face of God

Examples of 'amateur sociology' could be taken from the works of many contemporary theologians, but for the moment one further work will be sufficient. John Robinson's *The Human Face of God* provides an excellent example of a theologian-turned-sociologist in his analysis of 'four fundamental shifts' which he believes those studying christology must take into account. On the basis of this analysis, he argues that we must radically change our concepts in christology.

The first of the fundamental shifts which Robinson believes have taken place within contemporary society concerns 'modern man's' attitude towards 'myths':

> For men today, myth is equated with *un*reality. The mythical is the fictional. But in fact myth relates to what is deepest in human experience, to something much more primal and potent than the intellect. Psychologically and sociologically myth has been the binding force holding individuals and societies together. . . . Yet today myth cannot be taken as a description of how things did, do or will happen. For us it is an expression of significance, not an explanation for anything.[15]

My primary concern is not, surprisingly perhaps, with Robinson's confident sociological analysis of 'the binding force holding individuals and societies together'—most psychologists and sociologists would indeed be delighted if they *could* discover such a force—but rather with his proposal about what men do not believe today. It is possible that Robinson is simply making a semantic point— i.e. that in popular usage the term 'myth' refers to fictional stories. If that is so, then of course he is correct. But that hardly represents a 'fundamental shift' in contemporary thinking that has taken place in the last thirty years—and it is clear from the context of the quotation that Robinson *is* concerned with just such a shift. Is there really any evidence to suggest that a shift of this nature has occurred in the thinking of mankind or even in the thinking of Western mankind ? If there is sociological evidence to suggest this, then Robinson does not offer it.

It is possible, though, that the 'us' to whom Robinson refers is simply his fellow academics. Indeed, from the footnotes, it appears that he is referring to a small group of theologians who have been concerned to explore and develop Bultmann's concept of 'mythology'. If this is the case, then it is open to debate how far this group is representative of 'men today'. Robinson's second fundamental shift concerns 'metaphysics':

> What myth is to the imagination, metaphysics is to the intellect. It is the way of trying to state what is most real, most true, ultimate. One cannot, I believe, get away from metaphysics any more than from myth. It is concerned with how things are. Yet the meaningfulness of metaphysical statements in our day is equally problematic. Above all, confidence has gone in the type of supranaturalist ontology to which Christian theology in its classical presentation has been attached. According to this, what is 'really real' (*to on*) is located in another realm, above, beyond or behind phenomena. . . . Today this language has almost the opposite effect. A child of a friend of mine was heard saying in his prayers 'I'm sorry for you, God, up there while I am in the real world down here'. For we most naturally locate reality, not in another realm, but as the profoundest truth of this one.[16]

Again, it appears that Robinson has mankind in general— or, at least, Western mankind—in mind when he writes about this fundamental shift in thinking. And again, the sociologist must ask some awkward questions about evidence. Robinson is certainly presenting a sociological analysis at this point too— albeit an 'amateur' sociological analysis—since he is attempting to specify social change.

The only clear piece of evidence that he presents in this passage is the story about the child's prayer, which again may or may not reflect the rest of mankind. The sociologist would inevitably require a good deal of evidence before he could support Robinson's thesis—evidence that is patently lacking at present. Further, it is arguable, on the basis of our present sociological knowledge, either that Western man is indeed changing in his religious thinking or else that he has remained remarkably constant over the centuries. I will return to this theme in Part 3, when I consider the secularisation model at length. A number of possibilities, however, are open to those who wish to supply a sociological analysis of contemporary man's attitudes in the West towards metaphysics:

1. That metaphysics is becoming increasingly irrelevant—i.e. Robinson's thesis.
2. That metaphysics remains intelligible to most people, with the exception of the academic community.
3. That metaphysics has always been unintelligible to most people in most ages.

Even these three possibilities do not exhaust the list of viable alternatives—particularly if a sharp distinction is made between Western and non-Western peoples, or if it is assumed that no linear, monochrome trends vis à vis metaphysics are discernable within any society. Yet they at least show that those who wish to make an adequate analysis of contemporary thought must present serious sociological evidence to support their thesis.

Robinson's third shift concerns 'the demise of the language of the absolute':

> The classic way of expressing ultimate reality has been to use the vocabulary of uniqueness, of finality, of once-and-for-allness, of timeless perfection, of difference not merely of degree but of kind. Truth has been seen as unitary, rising like a Gothic arch and meeting in the One who is the answer to all possible questions. And it is not difficult to see how important a part this has played in Christian theology. Jesus Christ has been presented as *the* Son of God and Son of Man, and Alpha and Omega, in whom all lines meet, unique, perfect and final. Yet we live in a world of what Paul van Buren has called 'the dissolution of the absolute'. The monistic model has lost its power

51

over our thinking, whether about space or time. Ours is a relativistic, pluralistic world in which we are compelled to be more modest about our claims.[17]

Here it seems, at first at least, that Robinson is on firmer sociological ground. By introducing the concept of the pluralistic society, and by suggesting its possible effects to be a general relativising of claims to absolutism, Robinson can count on the support of a number of sociological theorists.[18] Certainly on *a priori* grounds it seems correct to assume, both that contemporary society in the West is becoming increasingly pluralistic, and that christological assertions of 'uniqueness' are consequently becoming more difficult to maintain. A pluralistic society, with a wide variety of competing faiths and claims to the truth, might well create the sort of shift that Robinson suggests.

Nevertheless, even at this point the sociological evidence is by no means unambiguous. Not all sociologists would agree that contemporary society in the West *has* become increasingly pluralistic.[19] Again, I shall return to this question in Part 3. Yet, even supposing that the West is becoming increasingly pluralistic, it still remains to be shown that contemporary man is becoming correspondingly more modest in his religious truth-claims. It is, of course, possible that he is, but this should be demonstrated rather than assumed.

It is, perhaps, only Robinson's final fundamental shift that avoids sociological difficulties. He argues that traditionally the Incarnation has been thoroughly rooted in history— 'traditional Christology has had a large and fairly crude stake in historicity'.[20] Today, though, New Testament critics are considerably less confident about the historicity of the Gospels than they were in earlier times: the so-called 'Jesus of history' has become a shadowy figure. At one point Robinson does in fact suggest that this attitude has now spread to 'modern man', but in general his comments are carefully confined to those academics who are concerned with studying the New Testament. It is precisely because he generally avoids statements about what contemporary man thinks or does, or about how vastly Western man as a whole has changed in the last thirty years, that he is able to avoid in this final point the sort of 'amateur sociology' that is so apparent in his other three points.

My two examples—Harvey Cox and John Robinson—might both be described as representatives of fairly radical theology. However, it will become apparent in Chapter 6, that it is not only radical theologians who tend to make rather sweeping and uncritical assumptions about Western society. In general, socio-theological correlations have been as yet remarkably unsophisticated.

The situation in contemporary theology might be paralleled with that in politics. David Martin argues that the sociologist can be useful to those concerned with political decision-making in several ways. In the first place, he can provide an analysis of the situation as it actually is, was or will be. And in the second place, he can trace both the antecedents of a situation and the possible future consequences of that situation. Of course, he cannot tell the politician what 'ought' to be done in a given situation—that is for politicians themselves and ethical commentators to say. But he can analyse the 'is', 'was', 'will be' or 'could be' of that situation—and, indeed, he is the person best qualified to do just that:

> These services which 'sociology' may provide represent the combined resources of economics, political science, etc., and are only new in that nowadays such services are explicitly sought and are systematically performed. Presumably in the past every politician and ethical commentator was an amateur political scientist and economist, more explicitly perhaps after Machiavelli in the European experience but implicitly everywhere and at all times. What is now understood in the multi-dimensional perspectives of sociology as systematised, verified propositional knowledge has always been practical knowledge, even if working with a 'Ptolemaic' rather than a 'Copernican' perspective'[21]

Martin's comments about politics, can, perhaps, be applied to theology. If theologians are to be concerned with the social context of theology—with the way people think within the particular societies in which they are operating—then they must expect to fail in their task if they ignore the critical perspective offered by sociologists. It would appear that theologians tend at times to write about 'what modern man thinks' or 'what urban man can accept'. However, when they do this, they are in effect acting as 'amateur sociologists'. Too often they ignore the work of the professional sociologist, and simply assume that they *know* what their fellow men think. It is possible that all that is happening is that they are dignifying their own thoughts by ascribing them to the rest of society.[22]

5

Plausibility Structures and Theology

BOTH HARVEY COX and John Robinson share a common belief.
Even though they present somewhat different analyses of
contemporary society, they are both convinced that such
analyses are highly relevant to theology. For both men some
form of socio-theological correlation is a *sine qua non* of the
theological perspective. In this chapter I will defend this basic
approach—though not, of course, the specific details of Coxs'
or Robinson's correlations which I criticised in the previous
chapter—and will examine the views of some of its critics.

By no means all contemporary theologians consider that the
findings of the sociologist are relevant to their enterprise.[1] In
his celebrated critique of Paul van Buren, John Knox and John
Robinson, Eric Mascall, for example, maintained that all three
theologians required that the Christian faith 'should be completely transformed in order to conform' to 'the outlook of
contemporary secularised man'.[2] Mascall clearly regarded such
a transformation as disastrous for theology. Apparently accept-
ing that a process of secularisation is indeed evident within the
West, he argued that Christianity should certainly not conform
to it:

> It reduces the dialogue between Christianity and contemporary
> thought to a purely one-way process; there is no question of
> contemporary thought adapting itself to the Gospel, the Gospel
> must come into line entirely with contemporary thought .... The
> contemporary man, they say in effect, is so radically secularised
> that he simply cannot accept supernatural Christianity; there-
> fore we must completely de-supernaturalise Christianity in order
> to give him something that he can accept.[3]

Mascall rejected this thesis, since it 'completely capitulates to
the outlook of the contemporary world', and, as a result, 'it has
no criterion for passing judgement on it.'[4]

For Mascall, then, a legitimate role for theology is to pass judgement on, or even effectively ignore, its social context. He is not concerned simply with the tendency of theologians like Cox or Robinson to conflate sociological descriptions with theological prescriptions. Rather, he is offering a critique of socio-theological correlations in general. If contemporary man cannot accept the claims of the Gospel, then it is contemporary man who must change, not the Gospel. Elsewhere Mascall admits that it may be necessary to review particular theological images at times—though even here he argues that urban dwellers, for example, are still capable of adopting rural images such as the shepherd simply because they are imaginative human beings.[5] The substance of the Gospel, however, must remain unchanged.

A number of crucial issues are involved in this debate. In the first place, there is radical disagreement amongst contemporary theologians about what does or does not constitute the 'substance of the Gospel'. Secondly, there is disagreement about the extent to which theology should pronounce judgement on contemporary thinking. And thirdly, there is disagreement about how seriously theology should take its social context. Important as all these issues are, however, it can only be the third which is of concern here.

From the perspective of this third area of disagreement, it is possible that if Mascall's approach were rigorously followed theology would largely fail to communicate with contemporary man. Thus, if theology is to ignore its social context, unless it is pronouncing judgement upon it, then it must expect to appear increasingly irrelevant within the society it is operating. In sociological terms, the relevance of contemporary theology is dependent, in part at least, on its adaptability to contemporary plausibility structures.

This claim clearly demands an understanding of both the nature of 'plausibility structures' and their relevance to the theological perspective. Peter Berger describes 'plausibility structures' as follows:

> One of the fundamental propositions of the sociology of know-
> ledge is that the plausibility, in the sense of what people actually
> find credible, of views of reality depends upon the social support
> these receive. Put more simply, we obtain our notions about
> the world originally from other human beings, and these notions

continue to be plausible to us in a very large measure because others continue to affirm them. . . . It is, of course, possible to go against the social consensus that surrounds us, but there are powerful pressures (which manifest themselves as psychological pressures within our own consciousness) to conform to the views and beliefs of our fellow men.[6]

Plausibility Structures

'Plausibility structures', then, are not simply societal assumptions or presuppositions. They are the implicit ways in which particular societies and groups within society distinguish between what is 'true' and what is 'false': they refer to socially determined structures of verification and falsification. An essential feature of this notion is that societies and groups within society do in fact differ in their appreciation of what is 'plausible' and what is 'implausible'.

Berger does not, of course, specify the extent to which societal plausibility structures are socially conditioned. He merely suggests that this conditioning is 'in a very large measure'. As I argued in Chapter 3, the sociologist is committed as a sociologist to an 'as if' methodology of social determinism. It is on methodological grounds, then, that he assumes that societal plausibility structure are socially determined. Nevertheless, it is possible to demonstrate even to the non-sociologist that plausibility structures do differ from society to society—and to suggest the very real possibility that particular plausibility structures are dependent, to some degree at least, on the social support they receive.

Even a brief examination of the trinitarian and christological debates of the early Church suggests that there were radical differences between the Latin-speaking and the Greek-speaking Christians. So for example, amongst the Latin-speakers the word *substantia* was used to denote the 'oneness' element of the trinitarian model, whereas amongst the Greek-speakers the word *hypostasis* was used to denote the 'threeness' element. Yet, etymologically the two words *substantia* and *hypostasis* derive from the same source. It seems clear, then, that the Western Christians were faced with problems rather different from those of the Eastern Christians. Whereas the latter were concerned to combat polytheism within their own society, the former

57

were not. As a result, the Latin-speakers could quite confidently use the term *persona* to denote the 'threeness' element, without being suspected of tritheism. Different social factors thus helped to create different concepts and plausibility structures.

A more recent example might be taken from contemporary religious attitude questionnaire-surveys. Twenty years ago such surveys often asked the simple question 'Do you believe in God?', without attempting to establish what sort of 'God' people believed in. Contemporary surveys, however, tend to be more sophisticated. So, one recent survey,[7] having established whether or not the interviewee believed in God, asked ',When you think of God, do you see him as "A Person" or "Some kind of impersonal power?"'. In this particular British survey, the responses to this question suggested that, whereas 80 per cent of the sample said that they were 'certain there is a God' or that they believed 'there is a God', though they were not certain, only 37 per cent of the sample actually thought that God was 'A Person'.

Even the question in this form, though, is hardly sophisticated, since many 'liberal' Christians might have a problem giving an unequivocal answer to the question 'Do you think God is "A Person"?' Several researchers have claimed that a far more complex series of questions is necessary in a questionnaire-survey to allow for differing types of belief.[8] Nevertheless, most of the respondents in the sample seemed able to cope with the choice presented in the question.

However, the same question within a different social context produced chaotic results. In a survey of Anglican theological students in Papua New Guinea, a highly confused pattern of answers emerged when I employed the question. On analysis it transpired that the students, all of whom were ordinands and spoke English well, found it difficult to distinguish between the alternatives suggested. For them the notion of 'impersonal power' was strange, since they considered that no 'spirit' or 'power' could really be 'impersonal': they made little attempt to divide phenomena into the 'personal' and the 'impersonal'. A distinction that presented comparatively few problems for the British was highly perplexing for the Papua New Guinean.

The difference between these two sets of thought-forms, though, is more fundamental than an ability or inability to make certain distinctions. The concept of plausibility structures suggests that the way a Papua New Guinean might test reality could be totally different from the way someone within the West might typically do so. Whereas those who live in the technological West might tend to test reality empirically, those who live in Papua New Guinea might tend to test reality through 'spirit directed' means of one sort or another. The Papua New Guinean, for example, who becomes actively involved in a Cargo Cult, is clearly working in a different causal system from the scientist who is conducting an experiment in the West.

This point is amply illustrated by the Papuan politician Albert Maori Kiki's account of his childhood experiences of 'cargo cults':

> Our own version of the cargo cult sprang up after the Second World War, with the return of ex-servicemen from the battlefield or the prisoner of war camps. Of course the notion had long persisted among our people that there was an island somewhere between Australia and Papua where the white man diverted all the cargo that was intended for us. Our own dead were sending us ships with axes, weapons, tinned food and clothes, but the white man had this magic and it enabled him to intercept these boats and change the labels. Thus the cargo intended for *Hare*, went to Mr Harry instead. The cargo intended for *Kave* went to Mr Cave instead, and so on. In 1945 a man called Larikapu appeared on Orokolo. He told us that when he was carried away by the Japanese into captivity he saw our dead relatives and they had shown him where our cargo was hidden. All that we had to do was raise the money to buy a boat to go and get it. Nobody doubted his word then, and we all contributed money. Of course the boat was never bought and the man disappeared from the village, and although our people knew he was living in Moresby, they never bothered to challenge him seriously and never attempted to recover their money. Nor did this experience make us any wiser. [9]

Two more 'prophets' quickly replaced Larikapu and the villagers again gave money and were deceived. In terms of the sociology of knowledge, it is apparent that the villagers and the 'prophets' were operating with widely differing plausibility structures. The former still lived in a thoroughly spirit-dominated world in which Western 'cargo' could only come from the spirits. The 'prophets', though, seemed to be aware that this was not the case.

Kiki also recalls the villagers' attitudes to the Japanese during the war. Although they never actually encountered the Japanese, they were not keen to help the Allies fight against them. The reason for this is obvious; the villagers were quite convinced that the Japanese were really their own ancestors' spirits, and that the Allies were trying to prevent them from bringing in the 'cargo'. So, by fighting the Japanese, the villagers would in effect be fighting their own ancestors.

The thought-patterns in this example are so strange to Westerners that the story simply appears to be ludicrous. Yet, for the Papuan villagers there was clearly nothing ludicrous or 'implausible' about it. For them it was the Westerner's explanation about tinned meat coming from factories which was ludicrous. Kiki's own ideas only changed when he actually saw such factories. Equally ridiculous to the Papuan villager was the Westerner's dismissal of the possibility that the Japanese could be the spirits of ancestors. At both of these points there was a direct confrontation of opposing plausibility structures. Further, the insistence of the Westerner that the Papuan was wrong merely tended to confirm in the latter's mind that he had something to hide. Thus, those implicitly assuming one type of plausibility structure naturally found the logic of others assuming a different plausibility structure thoroughly deficient.

Theology and Contemporary Plausibility Structures

Berger argues that contemporary plausibility structures are actually antagonistic towards Christianity, since there is evident a process of secularisation in the West. His overall argument is very similar to that of Mascall: both men believe that the West is characterised by secularisation and that the role of theology is to oppose it. For Berger, the contemporary situation may be depicted as follows:

> The proposition of the demise of the supernatural, or at least of its considerable decline, in the modern world is very plausible in terms of the available evidence. It is to be hoped that more plentiful and more precise evidence will yet be produced, and that there will be greater collaboration between social scientists and historians in this undertaking. But even now we have as

good an empirical foundation for the proposition as we do for most generalisations about our world. Whatever the situation may have been in the past, *today* the supernatural as a meaningful reality is absent or remote from the horizons of everyday life of large numbers, very probably of the majority, of people in modern societies, who seem to manage to get along without it quite well.[10]

I shall be examining Berger's account of the secularisation model at length in Chapter 7. For the moment, though, it is worth noting an obvious inconsistency in this quotation. Berger clearly regards secularisation as a process, that is a *historical* process. Further, it is apparent from other contexts,[11] that he believes that it is a process which is likely to continue into the future. Nevertheless, he argues for such a process from a single moment of time—the present. Whatever the weaknesses of this argument, though, it is important to note that Berger, like Mascall, accepts that there is a process of secularisation evident in the West today.

Within this situation of secularisation, Berger suggests that Christians inevitably become a 'cognitive minority'. In effect they become 'a group of people whose view of the world differs significantly from the one generally taken for granted in their society'.[12] They become a group possessing a body of 'deviant knowledge': that is, a group which no longer shares many of the plausibility structures of society at large.

Berger is aware, of course, that the depiction of Christianity in terms of 'deviance' does not affect its validity.[13] I have already argued in Chapter 2 that it is a mistake to confuse origins and projections with validity. Nevertheless, as a Christian he appears to be somewhat uneasy about the 'deviant' role he proposes for Christianity within a secularised society. Again this is understandable, perhaps, in the light of my suggestion that, although there is no logical link between origins, projections and validity, there may at times be a psychological link.

His initial solution was to make a somewhat Barthian dichotomy between 'religion' and 'Christianity'.[14] Having made such a dichotomy, the fact that the world rejects 'religious' thinking today is only partially relevant to Christianity. The latter is effectively immunised from trends affecting religious culture in general, including, perhaps, the process of secularisation itself.

However, he soon rejected this essentially theological, rather than sociological, dichotomy. In place of this solution to the problem of Christianity's deviant role within contemporary, secularised society, Berger now suggests that the Christian could 'relativise the relativisers'. More specifically, he proposes that Christians should apply the same socio-historical canons to contemporary plausibility structures that they applied to the plausibility structures of past generations:

> It may be conceded that there is in the modern world a certain type of consciousness that has difficulties with the supernatural. The statement remains, however, on the level of the socio-historical diagnosis. The diagnosed condition is *not* thereupon elevated to the status of an absolute criterion; the contemporary situation is not immune to relativising analysis. We may say that contemporary consciousness is such and such; we are left with the question of whether we will assent to it.[15]

The similarity of Berger's views to those of Mascall can now be clearly seen. Berger suggests that, although the Christian must recognise his 'deviant' role within contemporary, secularised society, he should not thereby be deterred from criticising this society. He is not obliged to conform to contemporary plausibility structures: instead, he may sit in judgement upon them.

Despite the obvious appeal of Berger's solution to the problem of the Church's role as a 'deviant body', it faces certain serious criticisms. Three weaknesses, in particular, might be isolated. The first of these relates to the accuracy of his analysis of contemporary religiosity, the second to the consistency and viability of his theological proposals, and the third to the role he allots to the Christian within contemporary society.

The first of these weaknesses, then, relates to Berger's initial sociological analysis. The problem of secularisation is crucial to any account of the social context of theology, and will indeed dominate discussion in succeeding chapters. If there is a process of secularisation evident within the West today, then it must have a radical effect on the whole theological enterprise. This remains the case whether particular theologians choose to ignore, challenge or accept this process. Even if secularisation is viewed, not as a process, but as a perennial condition of mankind, the theologian is still obliged to respond. So, if, as

Berger contends, people in the West today simply cannot make sense of supernatural claims, then this would clearly be a significant finding for theologians who are committed to such claims. Further, it would remain a significant finding even if it could be shown that mankind in general never could make sense of supernatural claims.

It will become apparent in Part 3, however, that such attempts to depict a process (or even permanent state) of cultural secularisation must face a number of sociological critics. Whether or not Berger's analysis is in the end accepted, it remains an obvious weakness of it that it ignores these critics.

The second weakness in Berger's thesis concerns his theological proposals. These have been criticized elsewhere[16] and are not of central importance here. It is sufficient to note, perhaps, that Berger's notion of 'signals of transcendence', which he offers for theology to pursue, is confronted with at least two difficulties. On his own argument it is not easy to see why these 'signals' should be viewed as anything other than human projections. They are not, of course, thereby invalidated, but presumably one would require some reason for believing that they are genuinely 'transcendent'. Further, even if he could establish that these 'signals' might be something other than human projections, he must still establish the validity of Christianity itself. Berger evidently has an implicit *a priori* belief in the centrality of Christianity.[17]

However, it is the third criticism which is the most crucial. If Berger's thoroughgoing secularisation model is correct, then it is clear that Christians may be forced into a highly 'deviant' role within contemporary society. If indeed they must refuse to compromise or relativise Christianity in any way—and both Berger and Mascall would maintain that this is essential—then their own plausibility structures will inevitably differ very widely from those of society as a whole. Given that this is the situation, it becomes difficult to see how the Christian is to communicate effectively with the non-Christian, and vice versa.

It is unnecessary, of course, to claim either that theology must be totally dependent upon contemporary plausibility structures, no matter how inhospitable these may be to religious belief, or that it can *never* sit in judgement upon them. Such claims would amount to an assumption that theology must

63

always act as a dependent, and never as an independent, variable within society. This would thoroughly undermine the interactionist approach to theology that I supported in Chapter 1. I believe that it is important to see theology as both influenced by, and as an influence upon, society at large; only such an approach does justice to the empirical evidence.

Nevertheless, my critisism of both Berger and Mascall is that they appear to believe that the Christian can effectively ignore contemporary plausibility structures and still expect to communicate with his fellow men. If, however, the Christian really does reject these plausibility structures in this wholesale manner, he must expect to become largely unintelligible to his non-Christian contemporaries. Such indeed would seem to be the situation amongst some sectarian Christians within the West: communication with certain introversionist sectarian members *is* extraordinarily difficult.[18] In practice, of course, few Christians really do 'relativise the relativisers' in any thoroughgoing manner, no matter how much they may disagree with the 'accepted wisdom' of their age.

Hermeneutics and Plausibility Structures

An adequate understanding of the social context of theology can no longer be viewed as a dispensable luxury. It appears rather to be a *sine-qua non* of a theology which communicates effectively with contemporary society. Berger and Mascall's cavalier dismissal of hermeneutics would not seem to be substantiated by an adequate understanding of plausibility structures in relation to theology. Some form of hermeneutics— whatever the theological difficulties may be—would appear to be essential in any age of theology.

It is interesting to note that two such different theologians as Leonard Hodgson and Karl Rahner agree on this point at least. In his Gifford Lectures, the former wrote:

> Nowhere within creation is there to be found any attempted statement of truth which is not coloured, and possibly miscoloured, by the outlook of its authors. Those who seek to set up as ultimate rival authorities the words of the Bible, the judgments of the Pope, the decrees of Church Councils or the utterances of saints or scholars, all agree in arguing from the same false premise.[19]

64

Somewhat similarly Rahner wrote:

> Anyone who takes seriously the 'historicity' of human truth . . .
> must see that neither abandonment of a formula nor its preser-
> vation in a petrified form does justice to human understanding.[20]

Once the theologian takes seriously the notion proposed by
sociologists of knowledge that 'language', 'knowledge' and
'plausibility structures' are all—in part at least—human pro-
ducts, he is faced with the problem of hermeneutics. Certainly
this sociological notion does not invalidate the theological
pursuit, but it *does* affect it.

The much-disputed theological methods of both Bultmann
and van Buren at least took this point seriously. However one
ultimately assesses Bultman's programme of 'demythologising',
or however confused one might feel his concept of 'mythology'
to be,[21] it primarily stemmed from a concern that twentieth-
century Christians cannot think in the same terms as first-
century Christians, and that they would fail to communicate
effectively with either 'outsiders' or themselves if they tried to
do so.

The hermeneutical context is crucial to an adequate understanding of Bultmann's celebrated claim that 'myth should
be interpreted not cosmologically, but anthropologically, or
better still, existentially',[22] when he had already defined' mythology' in a foot-note as 'the use of imagery to express the other
worldly in terms of this world and the divine in terms of this
life'.[23] His early critics at once accused him of theological
reductionism—of reducing theology to 'mere philosophy'.[24]
However, the fact that Bultmann continued to write about
'acts of God',[25] for example, should have been sufficient to
convince his critics that he was no simple reductionist. Instead,
he was attempting, albeit inadequately perhaps, to interpret
theology within the contemporary social context, that is, he
was taking hermeneutics seriously.

Similarly, Paul van Buren's attempt to provide 'the secular
meaning of the gospel' was a serious attempt to interpret
Christianity in the light of the contemporary social context.[26]
It was precisely because he took contemporary philosophical
thought seriously, and in particular the problem of verification,

that he attempted to re-express Christianity in terms of 'contagious freedom' without reference to God. He argued at the time that this concept both adequately described how Jesus thought about himself and could make sense of doctrines other than just christology. He admitted later, of course, that he had underestimated the centrality of God-language both in Jesus' own thought and in Christianity as a whole.[27] Nevertheless, at the time he considered the radical experiment of interpreting Christianity without reference to God to be necessary in view of the contemporary social context.

It is possible that the major error of both Bultmann and van Buren was not so much their theological interpretations—for which they have both been constantly criticised—as their implicit analyses of their social context. The paramount role that Bultmann assigns to scientific methodology (a thoroughly inductive understanding of this methodology) in contemporary society may do less than justice to his social context. His programme of 'demythologising' was based in effect on a thoroughgoing secularisation model, with all its attendant weaknesses. Paul van Buren, on the other hand, was dependent on logical positivism at a time when it was already giving way to functional analysis within philosophy. In addition, even when logical positivism was at its zenith in philosophy, it may or may not have represented the plausibility structures of society at large. Current philosophical trends may not necessarily be an accurate guide to contemporary social context.

Throughout history the Church has run the risk of translating the Gospel into different languages, thought-forms and plausibility structures. Doubtless there is always a risk of theological distortion involved in this process of translation—as there was, for example, when Christianity was originally translated from Judaic to Hellenistic thought-forms. Yet this risk may have been necessary for the survival of Christianity: without translation it would have failed to communicate effectively with others. Similarly, theology itself may become increasingly irrelevant to the society in which it is set if it ignores its social context. Much depends, of course, on an adequate analysis of the thought-forms and plausibility structures of contemporary society.

6

Societal Assumptions in a Theological Debate

IN THE previous chapter I argued that contemporary plausibility structures are highly relevant to theology, and that the latter ignores its social context only at the cost of jeopardising effective communication. In practice, however, most theologians do appear to make assumptions about contemporary society, and about the social context within which they pursue their discipline. I will return in this chapter to these assumptions—and, in particular, to some of the societal assumptions that are apparent in the *Honest to God* debate during the 1960s.

I have argued elsewhere[1] that this debate is of peculiar interest to the sociologist of religion partly because of its impact on the theological world, but mainly because of its effect on the non-theological world. A theological debate seldom moves outside the academic community, but, for a variety of reasons, the *Honest to God* debate drew an extraordinary number of people into its orbit. Whatever its theological merits or demerits it is certainly relevant to the sociological perspective.

Within this debate assumptions about the nature of society's attitudes towards religion played a significant role. In particular, the notion of secularisation was of central importance, with both defenders and critics of *Honest to God* making assumptions about a supposed process of secularisation in the West. Consequently, in this chapter I will examine the way some of the theologians involved in the debate employed this model. This will both serve to illustrate how theologians in practice analyse their social context, and strengthen the hypothesis of Chapter 4 that a considerably higher degree of sophistication is needed in the theological community concerning socio-theological correlations.

The secularisation model has been one of the most dominant societal models in recent theology, and may remain such for some time in the future.² It is not, of course, the only societal model that has been employed, but it remains the most widespread. Accordingly it forms an obvious choice of theme in this chapter. Nevertheless, it will again be clear that my aims are primarily methodological. I do not intend to give an exhaustive account of societal models and assumptions apparent in recent theology, even if such an account were possible. Instead the *Honest to God* debate, and the notions of secularisation evident within it, is offered solely as a case-study.

Preliminary Distinctions

In the next three chapters I will be concerned with a more detailed examination of the secularisation model from the sociological perspective. For the moment, however, it is necessary to make some preliminary distinctions in order to provide an adequate frame-work for analysing theologians' societal assumptions. More accurate definitions within this framework will emerge later, but here I will distinguish between secularisation models which refer to various dimensions of individual religiosity and those which refer instead to specifically cultural or socio-structural aspects.

At the individual level, Glock and Stark distinguish five core dimensions of religiosity.³ Firstly, there is the 'belief dimension'. This 'comprises expectations that the religious person will hold a certain theological outlook, that he will acknowledge the truth of the tenets of the religion'. Secondly, there is the dimension of 'religious practice'. This 'includes acts of worship and devotion, the things people *do* to carry out their religious commitment', and comprises both corporate ritual and solitary prayer. Thirdly, there is the 'experience dimension'. This 'takes into account the fact that all religions have certain expectations, however imprecisely they may be stated, that the properly religious person will at some time or another achieve a direct, subjective knowledge of ultimate reality; that he will achieve some sense of contact, however fleeting, with a supernatural agency.' Fourthly, there is the 'knowledge dimension'. This 'refers to the expectation that religious persons will possess some minimum of information about the basic tenets of their faith and its rites, scriptures and traditions'. And finally, there is the 'consequence dimension'. This 'identifies the effects of religious belief, practice, experience and knowledge in persons' day-to-day lives'.[4]

This analysis of religiosity, however, is not without weaknesses: the 'experience' and 'consequence' dimensions in particular have been criticised. So, for example, Roland Robertson argues that the first 'would appear very difficult to handle satisfactorily in the survey context, in so far as the sociologist is seeking to tap the depth and scope of the individual's religious emotionalism'.[5] Concerning the second, he maintains that, 'important as this theme is, it is difficult to see how in any logical sense one may be permitted to include within a scheme of dimensions of religiosity a dimension which is a consequence of religiosity . . . something cannot be both an aspect of x and at the same time a consequence of x'.[6] He also points out that for Glock and Stark the 'belief dimension' does not take into account 'degrees' of belief.

Nevertheless, the broad outline of this analysis may still be employable in the present context. The 'consequence' dimension of individual religiosity may or may not be a true dimension, but it remains relevant to the secularisation model. Again, the 'experience' dimension may well be difficult to handle in surveys, but it is still clearly relevant. Finally, the 'belief' dimension is also relevant, whether or not it is susceptible to analysis by 'degrees'—since secularisation theorists often claim that people today reject religious beliefs *in toto*. In any case, Robertson may simply be wrong in his criticism at this point: Glock and Stark *do* provide continua of beliefs.[7]

It is possible, though, that at the socio-structural level this analysis is inadequate. Again, Robertson argues:

We come . . . to the problem of the relationship between the religiosity of the individual and the religiosity of the system of which the individual is a member. Glock has argued that the 'religiousness of a society is subject to measurement through aggregating indicators of the religiosity of its constituent members'. It is on the other hand widely recognised in the social sciences that this kind of reasoning commits what is often called the *individualistic fallacy*. It is fallacious because one is viewing the system as no more than the sum or aggregation of the properties of the units within it.[8]

He points out that religiosity is not usually considered to be the same in Russia as in Britain, 'yet the evidence that we have suggests a broadly similar pattern of commitment at the level of the individual'.[9] The existence of an 'anti-religious' dominant minority within a country may ensure that the latter does not operate on religious principles. Consequently, in so far as the problem of the relative religiosity of societies is a soluble one, we must pay attention to structural and general characteristics of the system as a whole—the degree of differentiation and autonomy of religious sectors in relation to other social sectors, the strategic location or otherwise of religious leaders, the relationship between religious groups and so on'.[10]

At this point, Robertson introduces a further distinction: cultural as distinct from socio-structural religiosity. Here too culture cannot be derived from aggregation—'even if we confine our attention to culture, the objection must be made that in estimating the degree of religiosity of a particular culture there is much more to consider than aggregate individual attributes; there is, for example, the religious content in art forms or in language, not to speak of distinctively non-religious culture, such as modern science'.[11]

These distinctions between individual, socio-structural and cultural forms of religiosity are all relevant to the secularisation model, and together form a preliminary analytical frame-work. The secularisation model itself might also be given a preliminary definition in terms of 'religious decline'. This is a minimum definition: it will be seen in Part 3 that considerably more elaborate definitions have been offered. Yet most definitions of secularisation presume that it is both a process and a phenomenon of decline.

One final distinction should also be made. Theologians who adopt a secularisation model may use it to mean a decline in Christianity or a decline in religion in general. If it is used to mean the latter, then this opens the whole question of the definition, not just of religiosity, but of religion itself. Unfortunately, as I will show in Chapter 8, there is no universally accepted definition of religion in sociology (or in theology), or even an accepted approach toward a definition.

In *Honest to God*[12] the secularisation model appeared very seldom, and then mainly in quotations from Bonhoeffer. In *The Honest to God Debate*, however, which followed swiftly afterwards, it featured prominently. In the latter John Robinson disagreed with a definition in terms of 'the great defection from Christianity', arguing instead that secularisation was 'essentially a modern phenomenon'.[13] For him 'secularisation stands among other things for a revolt against three ways of viewing the world, and probably four, which have been intimately bound up in the past with the presentation of the Christian gospel';[14] namely, rejections of 'the whole possibility of metaphysics as a meaningful enterprise', 'a supranaturalistic world-view', a 'mythological' world-view, and the notion of 'religion'.[15]

The first three correspond fairly closely to the 'fundamental shifts' depicted in *The Human Face of God*, which I criticised in Chapter 4. It is clear that they all concern, in particular, the belief dimension of individual religiosity. Robinson believed that there had been a radical change in the beliefs of the individual in the West, and even suggested that this had led him to distrust 'any proposition going beyond the empirical evidence'.[16] Nevertheless, he was not personally convinced that 'to be honest as a Christian and as a secular man one must, or indeed can, be shut up to such a complete refusal to speak of "God" or of how things ultimately "are"'.[17] Instead he suggested in effect that there had been a shift away from the belief dimension of individual religiosity and towards the experience dimension. Thus, 'theology is not making affirmations about metaphysical realities *per se*, but always describes an experienced relationship or engagement to the truth . . . "all theological statements are existential"'.[18]

His fourth contemporary form of rejection, that concerning the notion of 'religion', has implications beyond individual religiosity. He interpreted 'religion' in this context in Bonhoeffer's terms, and defined secularisation as 'the withdrawal of areas of thought and life from religious—and finally also from metaphysical—control, and the attempt to understand and live in these areas in the terms which they alone offer'.[19] He linked this withdrawal to both decline in ritual practice at the individual level and socio-structural decline, and possibly cultural decline:

> For secularism stands for the conviction that the circle of explanation and control in human affairs can and should be closed—one does not have to 'bring in God' to account for the weather, or the origins of the universe, or the soul, or the foundations of morality, or anything else.[20]

It is possible that an account of secularisation at the socio-structural and cultural levels in the West can be supported by more substantial sociological evidence than that at the level of individual religiosity. In the next chapter I will review some of the evidence to this effect proposed by Peter Berger and Bryan Wilson.

E.L. Mascall

As I have already argued, Mascall, despite his diametrically opposite theological orientation, implicitly accepted a secularisation model similar to that of Robinson. He too located the process of secularisation primarily at the level of individual religiosity, believing that it signified the 'irreligious' or 'unchristian'. So, for example, he claimed in passing that today 'the world is, in its outlook, radically irreligious',[21] and that 'secularism' had 'in effect superseded Christianity as the attitude to life of the greater number of civilised Europeans and Americans'.[22]

There is, however, also a cultural element to Mascall's societal assumptions. In criticising van Buren's claim that contemporary 'Godlessness' derived from linguistic philosophy, he suggested that 'the main cause is the continual impact upon the senses of a technocratic culture in which all the emphasis falls upon what man can do with things and hardly upon what they really are'.[23] By implication, Mascall apparently linked individual and cultural religiosity, and even argued that van Buren and Robinson were themselves a part of the process of secularisation in the West.

A.M. Ramsey

One of the clearest definitions of the secularisation model in the *Honest to God* debate was provided by Michael Ramsey.

His initial reaction was somewhat hostile to Robinson's views. However, by 1969 he admitted that these views had been important at the time, suggesting four 'assumptions which are sometimes avowed and sometimes half-consciously present' in 'secularism':

1. The *temporal* world is the only world which exists. Eternity is irrelevant and meaningless. There can be no ideas of human values which transcend realisation within time and history.
2. *Religion* is to be dismissed. It involves unscientific superstitions, and can contribute no authentic knowledge about the world. It has encouraged people to resist scientific progress, and the practice of prayer and worship draws into an unreal realm of phantasy energies which should go into the world's proper business.
3. Man's *knowledge* is based solely upon observable phenomena. Thus 'positivism', though not an inherent part of secularism, is very characteristic of it.
4. Finally, the secularist believes in the *autonomous man*. Man's own potentialities of knowledge and of the effective use of it will suffice for all man's needs. True, man has his frustrations, but his dignity lies in his power to overcome them, as he can and will through the right application of the sciences to his needs. Religion gives not help but hindrance as it keeps man in a state of puerile dependence and holds him back from his maturity.[24]

Ramsey pointed out that one must 'avoid exaggeration, for secularism by no means occupies the whole scene'—in both Britain and America 'much from the older traditions still survives and shows creative power'.[25] As evidence he cited the high level of church-going in the States and the 'degree of public interest in religious questions which is reminiscent of middle-class Victorian England', and in Britain the fact that 'very few people would call themselves atheists' and that the 'ethical tradition as it exists is a pattern derived from earlier Christendom'.[26] Yet, he added that 'the ethos of secularism is strong and contagious, and the efforts of Christian evangelism often meet what can seem to be an almost impenetrable mass of secular-mindedness'.[27]

Clearly, Ramsey too assumed that there was a process of secularisation apparent within the West. His first three criteria relate to the belief dimension of individual religiosity: in terms of them secularisation involves a belief that the temporal world is the only world which matters, a belief that religion involves unscientific superstitions and belief solely in the empirical. Doubtless, these three criteria are inter-related, and may, in practice, be somewhat difficult to distinguish. The fourth criterion though—secular man as autonomous man—may also involve the consequence dimension of individual religiosity. For autonomous man religion is no longer an important factor to be considered in decision-making.

Like Robinson, Ramsey stressed the importance of the experience dimension in contemporary individual religiosity:

> In the modern world the concern about *persons* has had a new kind of prominence. There is a new kind of realisation of the proposition, not in itself of course new, that 'people matter'. One sign of this is the vogue of existential philosophy with its insistence that truth is known not in ontological statements but in terms of personal self-realisation. Another instance of this is the widespread practical concern to help people who are in distress. Another instance, of a totally different kind, is the behaviour of those who, frustrated in the desire for personal fulfilment, are almost compulsively led to try to prove themselves by achievements in sex and violence. Much indeed of the 'people matter' urge is a kind of revolt from the depersonalising of industrial or technological existence, where the secular city fails to satisfy. And movements like the 'hippies' seem to be a revolt from an unsatisfactory established order, perhaps a sort of secular counterpart to the flights of the hermits to the desert in the fourth century. Modern man has built the secular city, and is restless within it.[28]

This correspondence between Ramsey and Robinson is interesting, even though the former restricted his analysis to the level of individual religiosity. He did not consider wider questions of socio-structural or cultural secularisation.

Leslie Newbigin

In complete contrast, Leslie Newbigin's contribution to the debate was primarily concerned with these wider aspects of the process of secularisation. He argued that 'the most significant fact about the time in which we are living is that it is a time in which a single movement of secularisation is bringing the peoples of all continents into its sweep'.[29] For him, there were two aspects to this process; unification and secularisation itself.

On the level of unification, Newbigin argued that a combination of jets and radio 'have put every part of the world into immediate contact with every other'.[30] So, 'even in the most primitive areas the bus, the radio and the bulldozer move inexorably in, and when the necessities of world war or world commerce dictate it, anything from the jungles of Papua to the ice fields of the Antarctic can be swiftly taken over and incorporated in the single entity which is the human civilisation of today'.[31] At a more profound level, he claimed that 'thinking men and women in every part of the world are now aware of belonging to a single history . . . negatively, they are aware of standing under the threat of a single disaster which could destroy human civilisation as a whole . . . positively (but here one can only speak more vaguely), they share increasingly common expectations about the future, about human rights, dignity, technological development— expectations which they know can only be fulfilled if they are sought for all nations together'.[32]

On the level of cultural secularisation, he maintained that 'mankind is not being unified on the basis of a common religious faith or even of a common ideology, but on the basis of a shared secular terror and a shared secular hope'.[33] Goals within the 'Third World' today are 'defined in such terms as technical development, industrialisation, economic planning, productivity and the more equal distribution of wealth'.[34] Potentially, at least, these goals could draw 'all races into common involvement in a single universe of thought as well as a single fabric of economic life':[35]

> Its effect (not recognised at first) is to destroy the cyclical pattern of human thinking which has been characteristic of many ancient societies and to replace it by a linear pattern, a way of thinking about human life which takes change for granted, which encourages the younger generation to think differently from its parents, which looks for satisfaction in an earthly future.[36]

At the socio-structural level, too, Newbigin argued that the process of secularisation had deeply affected a country like

India. Today, India is no longer 'determined by the traditional ideas of Hindu or Muslim law . . . Legislation has been passed which is aimed to destroy completely elements in traditional religious law which are considered incompatible with this intention.'[37] He maintained that in the contemporary secular state of India it has become increasingly irrelevant whether the individual is a Hindu or a Muslim. A similar process is also evident within the West:

> More and more areas of life have been mapped by the research of those who confessed that they did not need the hypothesis of God for this purpose; more and more of the life of society, of the family, of the individual—including the Christian individual; have been organised without any conscious reference to the Christian faith or the Christian Church.[38]

F. R. Barry

Finally, F.R. Barry provides an interesting example of one of the few theologians involved in the debate who explicitly employed, and showed a real acquaintance with, sociological accounts of the secularisation model. Most theologians contributing to the debate made assumptions about society and patterns of contemporary religiosity—whether at the individual, cultural or socio-structural levels. Some of them, like Ramsey and Newbigin, supported these assumptions with empirical evidence. But few of them actually referred to the work of sociologists of religion. Barry was an exception.

He concentrated on the specific area of the practice and belief dimensions of individual religiosity. He admitted, on the basis of the evidence he reviewed, that there had been some sort of decline in church-going in Britain during the last century. Yet he argued:

> Can it be assumed, for example, that in the Victorian age when social acceptance was bound up with church-going as at least a guarantee of respectability, there were more believers in God than there are today? Or even in the so-called ages of faith? (How Christian, in other words was Christendom?). Can we simply assume that because in the United States church membership embraces 65 per cent of the population, against

22 per cent in Britain, there are more believers in God in the United States than there are in Britain? . . . The real influence of a church in the life of its community, and especially such a church as the Church of England, cannot in the nature of the case be assessed by any numerical calculation.[39]

On the basis of the *Puzzled People* in Britain[40], Barry argued that there is evidence in the belief dimension of individual religiosity of 'the vestigial remainder of confused and muddled Christian tradition in a surprisingly large number of people'.[41] Without adopting a thoroughgoing secularisation model, he maintained that contemporary man in the West is 'ambivalent'. On the one hand 'the "modern" mind is indelibly empiricist with a frame of reference almost entirely bounded by facts that lie in the field of natural science, neutral facts which are the same for everybody. . . . There is no place in the contemporary world-view for transcendent or "supernatural" realities which do not admit of empirical verification or cannot be comprised in equations',[42] On the other hand, having made what appears to be a bland claim about society, he maintained that there is a 'vestigial remainder' of Christian tradition in society.

In both of these dimensions of individual religiosity Barry pointed to important ambiguities contained within the available sociological data. I shall return to these ambiguities in the final chapter.

The Debate Assessed

A number of weaknesses emerge from this brief survey of the societal assumptions of five of the theologians involved in the *Honest to God* debate. They all relate to issues which the critical perspective of sociological accounts of secularisation might have remedied, since a common factor of all the weaknesses is a tendency on the part of the theologians to make uncritical assumptions about the nature of contemporary society. At the very least the discipline of academic sociology exists to challenge such assumptions.

The first and most obvious of these weaknesses is that none of the theologians in question supplied a comprehensive secularisation model. In terms of my preliminary frame-work, all excluded one or other of the dimensions of secularisation that have been suggested by sociologists of religion. In contrast to the thoroughgoing secularisation models of Berger and Wilson that I will examine in the next chapter, those provided by the five theologians must appear narrow and limited. Thus, Barry concentrated solely on the individual level of secularisation, and in particular on the dimensions of belief and practice: at no point did he refer to more broadly-based understandings of secularisation. Ramsey too concentrated on this level of secularisation, though he included references to the experience and consequence dimensions of individual religiosity in addition to the two studied by Barry. Both Robinson and Mascall alluded to the socio-structural and cultural levels of secularisation, but they too focussed upon the process as an individual-oriented phenomenon. Thus, the first concentrated upon secularisation as a process related to the belief and experience dimensions of individual religiosity, whereas the second was concerned solely with the belief dimension. In contrast to the other theologians, however, Newbigin referred only to the socio-structural and cultural levels of secularisation.

Focussing upon certain elements of the secularisation model, of course, is not in itself inaccurate. It only becomes so if the focus is taken to constitute the whole. Both theologians and sociologists may legitimately concentrate upon certain features of the secularisation model, provided they are aware that others have suggested other features too. Lacking a sufficiently critical understanding of the model, however, it would seem that the five theologians in question were not so aware.

This lack of awareness may relate to the second weakness apparent from my survey—namely, the lack of a critical definition of secularisation on the part of the theologians. Only Ramsey provided a systematised definition of secularisation— and even this lacked the critical perspective that might have been provided by the sociologist. Robinson also made four suggestions about the nature of secularisation, but these in themselves do not provide a systematised definition, nor again do they contain a critical perspective. Mascall, on the other hand, simply assumed that a process of secularisation exists, and nowhere attempted to give it a formal definition. Not one of the theologians, it should be noted, adopted any of the formal definitions of secularisation provided by sociologists of religion.

The final weakness relates to the unwillingness of the theologians to substantiate their claims with empirical data. Admittedly, some of this data became more widely available towards the end of the decade, but it would appear to be the case, as I argued in Chapter 4, that theologians such as Robinson make societal assumptions even today without reference to it. Most noticeably, the only data that Mascall employed systematically related to his fellow theologians. For him Robinson, Knox and van Buren were in themselves evidence of a process of secularisation. Nowhere, though, did he give the same attention to more obvious empirical evidence for such a process. Ramsey did refer to some of this data, but again he lacked the sort of critical perspective expected by the sociologist. Newbigin too lacked this perspective, though he did allude to a wide range of empirical evidence for socio-structural and cultural types of secularisation. Only Barry, it would appear, systematically employed the data provided by sociologists of religion on individual religiosity.

At each point, then, it would seem that the theologians might have benefited from a greater awareness of the findings of the sociologist of religion. In the succeeding chapters I will be critical at times of the work of the latter, but such criticism does not undermine the relevance of these findings to the theological enterprise. Rather it may serve to underline the need for a thoroughly critical perspective in socio-theological correlations.

PART THREE

Societal Plausibility Structures

7

The Thoroughgoing Secularisation Model Amongst Sociologists

IN THE previous section I have argued at length that the theologian cannot afford to ignore the social context within which he works. Some form of hermeneutics is essential for all those theologians who wish to communicate with their fellow men. This much, at least, seems to be demanded by any serious understanding of the role of plausibility structures within our language and thought-forms.

However, in practice, as has also been argued, theologians today do not usually ignore their social context. Instead they often appear to have strongly held views about the nature of the society in which they live—though, sadly, not always views which can be substantiated by sociological analysis. Further, in making statements about the nature of contemporary society or about that oft-mentioned 'modern man', they do not always seem to be aware that they are in effect becoming 'amateur sociologists' in the process.

Of course this criticism does not just apply to theologians. Many social commentators are equally prone to making unsubstantiated claims about the nature of the society in which they live. So, for example, two of the most widely-read 'social prophets' of the previous decade, Herbert Marcuse and Marshall McLuhan, were both attacked for just this reason. The latter's claim that society is 'shaped more by the nature of the media by which men communicate than by the content of the communication',[1] has been criticised precisely on empirical grounds, since it is indeed an empirical claim.[2] Further, British research into the effects of the mass media upon society would seem to count against the accuracy of this claim.[3]

In his celebrated critique of Marcuse, Alasdair MacIntyre concluded that:

Marcuse seldom if ever, gives us any reason to believe that what he is writing is true. He offers incidental illustrations of his theses very often; he never offers evidence in a systematic way. Above all there is entirely absent from his writing any attempt on his own part to suggest or to consider the difficulties that arise for his positions and hence also no attempt to meet them.[4]

It must be remembered that at the time MacIntyre was writing Marcuse's views about the contemporary nature of 'one dimensional society', as he termed it, were often accepted enthusiastically and quite uncritically. MacIntyre's short study helped to place these views in a far more critical/empirical context.

Similarly, as I argued in Chapters 4 and 6 it is important to set the claims that theologians tend to make about contemporary society within a critical context. Too often in the past these claims have simply been ignored or else accepted without question. However, if the social context within which theologians work is relevant to contemporary theology, then it is clearly vital that only the most adequate analyses of that social context should be employed.

In the previous chapter it has been shown that the secularisation model has played an important role within contemporary theology. Of course, this model has not always been understood or interpreted in the same way by all theologians, but it still represents an important assumption amongst many theologians. Interestingly, the secularisation model (again understood in a variety of ways) has performed an important role within current sociology of religion. Amongst sociologists specialising in religious phenomena a fairly substantial body of literature has developed around the problem of secularisation and it will be the aim of this final section to examine some of this literature and to relate it to the social context of theology. It is curious, perhaps, that theologians and sociologists have tended to analyse this problem in the past with little reference to each other at this fruitful point of contact. My aim, of course, is primarily methodological: by examining the secularisation model I am not intending to claim that it is the only relevant model to the social context of theology. The examination of a single model will, though, serve to expose the means by which the theologian may discern this context.

The problem of secularisation, however, does not simply represent a fruitful point of contact between theology and sociology. It is also a crucial and wide-spread interpretative model of contemporary religiosity within urban, industrial society. So often sociology challenges popular conceptions, but at this point much of the sociology of religion seems to confirm them. If it is indeed a fairly wide-spread notion that 'religion is on the decline' within the West at least, then many thoroughgoing secularisation theorists would appear to be endorsing this notion and setting it within a theoretical context. Perhaps the persistence of secularisation theories even in the face of ambiguous empirical evidence owes something to this unusual correspondence between popular notions and sociological theory.

Berger's Secularisation Model

It has already been noted in passing that Peter Berger is a thoroughgoing secularisation theorist. His premise in *A Rumour of Angels* is that 'whatever the situation may have been in the past, *today* the supernatural as a meaningful reality is absent or remote from the horizons of everyday life of large numbers, very probably of the majority, of people in modern societies, who seem to manage to get along without it quite well'.[5] It is important to notice both that Berger seems to be concerned here only with the belief dimension of religiosity and that he ignores the historical problem altogether.

Within *The Social Reality of Religion*, however, Berger supplies a more comprehensive definition of the process of secularisation. He insists, despite the critics of the secularisation model, that this process can be expressed unambiguously and without ideological connotations, whether Marxist or Christian. It is not necessary for a sociologist as a sociologist to adopt an evaluative stance towards secularisation, but simply to describe it as a historical and contemporary process. As such he supplies the following definition:

> By secularisation we mean the process by which sectors of society and culture are removed from the domination of religious institutions and symbols. When we speak of society and institutions in modern Western history, of course, secularisation manifests itself in the evacuation by the Christian Churches

of areas previously under their control or influence—as in the separation of Church and state, or in the expropriation of Church lands, or in the emancipation of education from ecclesiastical authority. When we speak of culture and symbols, however, we imply that secularisation is more than a social-structural process. It affects the totality of cultural life and of ideation, and may be observed in the decline of religious contents in the arts, in philosophy, in literature and, most important of all, in the rise of science as an autonomous, thoroughly secular perspective on the world. Moreover, it is implied here that the process of secularisation has a subjective side as well. As there is a secularisation of society and culture, so is there a secularisation of consciousness. Put simply, this means that the modern West has produced an increasing number of individuals who look upon the world and their own lives without the benefit of religious interpretations.[6]

It has been necessary to quote this passage in full because it is the clearest and most comprehensive definition that Berger gives of the secularisation model. In fact it is an unusually broad definition since it covers, not simply individual religiosity, but also social-structures and culture in general. Further, it soon becomes apparent that this understanding of secularisation as a cultural process has historical roots spanning three thousand years. This is, perhaps, one of the boldest understandings of secularisation to be advanced by contemporary sociologists of religion.

Berger holds, it should be remembered, a strictly substantive definition of 'religion', viewing it as 'the human enterprise by which a sacred cosmos is established', and understanding 'sacred' as 'a quality of mysterious and awesome power, other than man and yet related to him, which is believed to reside in certain objects of experience'.[7] It is not surprising, then, that his interpretation of the secularisation of individual religiosity should focus upon the belief dimension, and in particular upon 'the secularisation of consciousness'. He suggests, however, that this form of secularisation has not been uniform even in the contemporary West. Citing in particular the work of the French 'religious sociologists', he claims that the impact of secularisation has tended to be stronger on men than on women, on those in their middle years, on urban dwellers, on the working class and on Protestants and Jews. Amongst these groups Berger sees clear evidence of a process of secularisation.

He is fully aware, though, that the empirical evidence from the States is somewhat different from that of Europe and Britain, since there 'the Churches still occupy a more central symbolic position'. Nevertheless, he still believes that there is a process of secularisation evident within the States. He argues that the American Churches 'have succeeded in keeping this position only by becoming highly secularised themselves, so that the European and American cases represent two variations on the same underlying theme of global secularisation.'[8]

Two points should be noticed about Berger's understanding of secularisation at this juncture as a process that affects individual religiosity. In the first place, there is something unhappy about his interpretation of the apparently very different sets of empirical evidence from the States and from Europe. Bowker's claim against Freud that 'all evidence that superficially appears to contradict the theory is converted to become evidence *for* the theory',[9] also seems to apply with some justice to Berger. A secularisation theory which is able to interpret evidence of both decline in individual religiosity in Europe and apparent increase, or at least persistence, in individual religiosity in the States, as equally counting for a process of secularisation must be suspect at least on grounds of non-falsifiability. Just what sort of empirical evidence would count against a theory of secularisation expressed in these terms? Berger does not help us.

In the second place, it is interesting that Berger explicitly refers to the evidence of the French 'religious sociologists' in his attempt to show patterns of secularisation in individual religiosity. However, this evidence high-lights the difficulties involved in attaining genuine evidence of individual religiosity. It is necessary for the moment to concentrate on the specifically methodological difficulties involved in interpreting this evidence.

F. Boulard's *An Introduction to Religious Sociology*[10] is, perhaps, the best known work in 'religious sociology', and in many ways it typifies the methodological problems involved in measuring or quantifying religiosity. Boulard concentrated upon rural France in his attempt to provide a 'religious map' for the Roman Catholic Church's missionary strategy. Prior to his research it had usually been assumed that the greatest variations in religiosity were to be found in a comparison of rural and urban situations. However, he sought to show that similar variations could be shown within rural situations themselves. Accordingly, he classified different parts of rural France on his 'religious map' into one of three categories (with a fourth for areas containing a significant number of Protestants). The first category consisted of those areas where at least 45 per cent of the population over the age of twenty made an Easter Communion and in principle attended Sunday Mass: the second of those areas where less than 45 per cent of the population did so, though there was still wide-spread 'seasonal conformity' (i.e. baptism, confirmation, marriage and burial): and the third where a minimum of 20 per cent of the population were not baptised and did not attend catechism.

The results of this method were quite startling. Boulard found that only the fringe rural areas far from the large industrial zones—Brittany, the Pyrenees, the Massif Central and the Jura—conformed to his first category. The central rural parts of France and various areas in the North and South all conformed to the other two categories, and in some cases closely matched urban industrial parts of the country. Interesting as these results were, however, they did suffer from certain fundamental weaknesses.

Most obviously, Boulard's research is usually criticised[11] because it is too church-centred and too dependent on church-going statistics. Despite his oft-repeated claim that all historical and social factors should be taken into consideration when one is attempting to describe the current religious situation of a particular country, in practice the majority of his research was based on statistics for church-attendance. In the context of a predominantly Roman Catholic country such as France this basis for research might be less misleading than it would be in a more denominational country, since in the latter it is by no means clear that 'going to Church' carries the same connotations for members of different denominations. Boulard himself realised that church-going was not always a good measure of individual religiosity. It is quite possible for the same individual to combine a high level of religious practice with a low level of religious belief or commitment.[12] Despite this obvious criticism Boulard still defended his methodology:

> Clearly religious practice is not the whole of religious vitality. Yet it is a sign the importance of which is not to be underestimated; the canons make attendance at Mass and performance of Easter duties obligatory, so that a man is not, in a strict sense, Christian, unless he practises his religion. In addition, this sign has the great advantage of being objective. If an incumbent takes the trouble to count those who came to Mass or those who make their Easter communion he can have accurate figures; and two successive incumbents in the same parish, who make the same count, can arrive at comparable figures.[13]

The first part of Boulard's argument—i.e. that a man is not a Christian unless he practises his religion—is really a theological not a sociological argument. It also assumes that a Christian must practise his religion *publicly*. The second part, however, is probably a utilitarian argument, since Boulard may have confused 'objectivity' with 'easiness'. Undoubtedly churchgoing statistics are comparatively easy to collect, but they may not be the best indicator of individual religiosity.

Berger's dependence on such evidence weakens his claims about the process of secularisation within individual religiosity in the West. There has indeed been a considerable amount of research into patterns of religious practice and a certain amount of research into patterns of religious belief, both in Europe and in the States, but this may or may not give an accurate picture of individual religiosity as such.

Even the comparatively sophisticated research methods of the ITA Survey *Religion in Britain and Northern Ireland*[14] do not wholly resolve this problem. This survey used nine variables in its religiosity scale, based on 'a combination of two kinds of factors, one indicating the importance of religion to the informant and the other kind indicating the extent to which the informant endorsed traditional Christian beliefs'.[15] The following variables were used—all based, of course, on the interviewees' responses:

1. They are 'very religious' or 'fairly religious'
2. They are 'certain' that to lead a good life it is necessary to have some religious belief

3. They are 'certain' that without belief in God life is meaningless
4. They are 'certain' that religion helps to maintain the standards and morals of society
5. They are 'certain' there is a God
6. They believe that 'God does watch each person'
7. They are 'very likely' to think of God when they are worried
8. They are 'very likely' or 'fairly likely' to think of God when they are happy
9. Their everyday lives are affected 'a great deal' or 'quite a lot' by their religious beliefs.[16]

A religiosity scale was developed from these nine variables by dividing the sample into the following four groups:

> None or 1 'religious' reply   — —
> 2,3, or 4 'religious' replies   —
> 5,6, or 7 'religious' replies   +
> 8 or 9 'religious' replies   + +

The survey was aware that 'a significant proportion of the population (including a substantial number of clergymen) might be very "religious", in that religion was very important to them, while endorsing very few of the traditional beliefs.'[17] In order to guard against this, the data from the nine variables were compared, and it was found that 'any informant who is classified as "religious" on one question' was in fact 'more likely than the average person to be "religious" on all other questions used in the scale'.[18]

However, even this comparative methodology does not remove all the difficulties involved in compiling a religiosity scale. It is presumably possible for an individual, who feels himself (variable 1) to be 'religious'—a term incidently that some will dislike—and who apparently features positively on the consequence dimension of religiosity (variables 7–9), to be unable to make 'certainty' claims on the belief dimension (variables 2–8). Such an individual would only merit a single minus grade on the ITA religiosity scale, as indeed he would on the Glock and Stark scale of 'orthodoxy' mentioned in the first chapter.[19]

An additional problem is created by the fact that this survey was only an attitude survey. It makes no attempt to measure people's stated behaviour against their actual behaviour. Doubtless this would be extraordinarily difficult to achieve, but it would still be a necessary procedure in any adequate examination of the consequence dimension of religiosity.

Finally, it should be noted that the survey is by no means exhaustive in its examination of dimensions of individual religiosity. In particular there is no attempt to measure the experience dimension, and even the belief dimension that it examines gives little indication of actual religious 'commitment'. The individual mentioned above who feels himself to be 'religious' and to be significantly affected by religious beliefs—and even to be a 'committed' religious believer—may still not be 'certain' about these beliefs. When surveys do make this confusion of religious 'certainty' with religious 'commitment', it may indeed matter little in the majority of cases, but amongst the more thoughtful these two notions may be very distinct. Claims of religious 'certainty' may be a better test of religious sectarianism than 'commitment'.[20]

Overall it is possible that the claim of Robertson and Campbell that 'we really know very little about the "inner-layers" of religious belief and experience'[21] is accurate. If this is the case then it seems likely that any religiosity scale at present is likely to be less than successful. Yet of course, the whole attempt to show patterns of secularisation in individual religiosity is itself dependent on the availability of an adequate religiosity scale. Berger does less than justice to this problem in citing empirical evidence that cannot bear the weight of his concept of individual secularisation.

When he moves to secularisation within social structures and culture, however, Berger does produce more evidence. He sees the secularisation of social structures mainly in the shift that has occurred, in most Western countries, of ecclesiastical control. So, in all but a few countries there has been, over the centuries, a separation between Church and state. Whereas once the churches controlled educational, medical and social agencies throughout Europe, today this is seldom the case. Even in Eire, one might add, the *ne temere* clause is becoming increasingly vacuous. Without doubt there is real historical evidence in Europe, at least, to suggest that ecclesiastical control has diminished since the Middle Ages—and, furthermore, that it continues to diminish.

Much of his argument, though, is devoted to more cultural aspects of the process of secularisation. He suggests that the purveyors of this form of secularisation are numerous, though they must include contemporary science, technology and media of communication—'today, it would seem, it is industrial society in itself that is secularising, with its divergent ideological legitimations serving merely as modifications of the global secularisation process.'[22] Without denying, however, that there are many possible explanations of this process, Berger specifically concentrates on 'the question of the extent to which the Western religious tradition may have carried the seeds of secularisation within itself.'[23] It is with this peculiarly cultural aspect of secularisation that he is basically concerned.

Berger argues that the central notion which is relevant at this point is that of 'disenchantment of the world'. This notion denotes a cultural process that is evident both in Protestantism and even in Judaism. Compared with Catholicism, Protestantism 'appears as radical truncation, a reduction to "essentials" at the expense of a vast wealth of religious contents', as 'an immense shrinkage in the scope of the sacred in reality', and as divesting itself 'as much as possible from the three most ancient and most powerful concomitants of the sacred—mystery, miracle and magic'.[24] Compared with the religions of Egypt and Mesopotamia, Judaism too posits a God who is 'radically transcendent, not to be identified with any natural or human phenomena', and who is 'not only the creator of the world but the *only* God—if not the only one in existence, at any rate the only one who mattered for Israel . . . unaccompanied by a pantheon of any sort.'[25]

This thoroughgoing understanding of cultural secularisation is far more sweeping than most understandings of the process, and herein may lie its main weakness. Berger is forced to make vast generalisations and finally to identify Catholicism in the West as a 'retrogressive step in terms of the secularising motifs of Old Testament religion'.[26] Inevitably, perhaps, such generalisations tend to treat history selectively. So, Berger ignores evidence even in later Judaism which might appear to compromise a strict understanding of transcendent monotheism, like the enigmatic figure of 'wisdom' in the wisdom literature of the Old Testament and Apocrypha. Further, like Weber, he possibly understands Protestantism in too Calvinistic terms—though even Calvin retained the sacraments of baptism and communion at the risk of 'mystery-' and 'miracle-' filled interpretations of them in the popular mind. It is possible that such 'historical sweeps' do less than justice to history.

None of these objections, of course, exclude the possibility that there has been a cultural process of secularisation within Protestantism and Judaism. It is possible that there has. However, it is difficult to see how such a process could be established without an extremely lengthy analysis of both forms of religion—both at the theological and popular levels. It is well known, within both Western and Eastern religions, that there is often a gap between the pronouncements of the 'orthodox' theologians and the beliefs of the popular participants. Yet Berger does not always observe this distinction in his analysis. However, any adequate understanding of secularisation, even at the general cultural level, must be aware of this distinction.

There might, however, be one way of establishing a cultural secularisation model at the popular level, though Berger does not employ it directly. This way would be on the basis of *a priori* argument rather than on empirical evidence. The latter is almost impossible to obtain since historical evidence usually relates to the literate minority in any given society and not to the non-literate majority within that society (it is obviously not possible to conduct a questionnaire-survey of popular attitudes and beliefs on our ancestors!). Nevertheless, an *a priori* argument based on the relationship between societal structures and popular beliefs is possible. For example, it might be argued that contemporary comparisons between Western urban, industrial societies and Third-world rural, village societies suggest that competing plausibility structures abound in the former. Whereas in the West we usually characterise our society as 'pluralist', even at the popular cultural level, we tend to ascribe a more monochrome world-view to so-called 'traditional' societies.

This *a priori* argument might continue that in the less 'pluralist' pre-industrial West one might expect to have found a more monochrome or unified world-view at the popular cultural level. Even though we lack any empirical evidence as such, we might suggest that the average pre-industrial Westerner would be less inclined to doubt the statements of the pre-Reformation Church than he would be today in a situation of cultural 'pluralism' and ecclesiastical denominationalism. Of course, such an argument could say little about religious 'commitment' as distinct from religious 'belief', amongst the majority of the population, since the existence of a unified world-view does not exclude the possibility of various types of commitment to this world-view. Yet it does at least suggest a way of identifying important differences between current and past popular religiosity.

Naturally, this *a priori* argument is not without difficulties, particularly in its use of such concepts as a 'pluralist' society and its assumption that current 'traditional' societies are in any way comparable to pre-industrial Western society. Further, it does not allow a would-be secularisation theorist to construct such a sweeping model as Berger suggests. However, I shall return to these difficulties in a later chapter.

Wilson's Secularisation Model

It is possible that Bryan Wilson is presenting a similar *a priori* argument in his seminal *Religion in Secular Society*.[27] Like Berger, Wilson has a thoroughgoing understanding of the secularisation model. He argues that 'religious thinking, religious practices and religious institutions were once at the very centre of the life of western society, as indeed of all societies'.[28] But today the situation is radically different:

> In the twentieth century that situation has manifestly changed, and the process of change continues. But change does not occur evenly, nor in necessarily similar ways in different societies. Religious *practice* may atrophy, as it has, for example, in Scandinavian countries; or it may persist in its traditional forms (and even become more extensive) whilst its social and cultural meaning changes, as in the United States. Religious *institutions* may also continue and show, as in America, remarkable resilience, but they may do so by transforming themselves from largely traditional styles to organisations which embody all the rational bureaucratic authority assumptions of other, non-religious, organisations in advanced society. Religious *thinking*

is perhaps the area which evidences most conspicuous change. Men act less and less in response to religious motivation: they assess the world in empirical and rational terms, and find themselves involved in rational organisations and rationally determined roles which allow small scope for such religious predilections as they might privately entertain. Even if, as some sociologists have argued, non-logical behaviour continues in unabated measure in human society, then at least the terms of non-rationality have changed. It is no longer the dogmas of the Christian Church which dictate behaviour, but quite other irrational and arbitrary assumptions about life, society and the laws which govern the physical universe.[29]

It is worth noting a number of weaknesses in this statement on the process by which religion has become increasingly 'epiphenomenal' in the West. As an understanding of secularisation it may be criticised in a similar way to that of Berger. For example, Wilson too apparently uses evidence of both decline in church-going and persistence, or even increase, in church-going to demonstrate a process of secularisation. He argues that 'it would require an ingenious sociological analysis to show that the development of American society was materially affected by its high rate of church-going, or that of Sweden by its very low rate'.[30] Yet, having argued this he immediately devotes a whole chapter to statistics of decline in the Church of England during this century. On his own presuppositions it should matter very little whether these statistics demonstrate decline, persistence or increase.

Another obvious weakness in Wilson's statement concerns his unsubstantiated claim that people today 'assess the world in empirical and rational terms'. He immediately compromises this claim with his subsequent admission that 'non-logical behaviour', albeit not related to the dogmas of the Christian Church, may continue 'in unabated measure in human society'. The effect of this admission is to produce doubts as to whether Wilson is really writing about secularisation at all. The term 'secularisation' presumably refers to 'religious' decline and not simply to a decline in Christianity, and yet Wilson's evidence is related almost entirely to the latter. Elsewhere he can even write about 'man's ambivalent hankering for magical and millenial solutions'[31] to problems in life within contemporary

Western society—whilst at the same time still maintaining a model of cultural secularisation. The very presence, though, of forms of religiosity in the West, which are not explicitly however church-oriented, must create doubt about the notion that people today 'assess the world in empirical and rational terms'.

Wilson seemingly comes close to making the assumption of identifying church and religion which Thomas Luckmann exposed, possibly on the methodological principle that 'religion may be many things, but it is amenable to scientific analysis only to the extent that it becomes organised and institutionalised'.[32] As a result of sociologists using this principle, Luckmann suggested that 'it need surprise no one that the historical and ethnological horizons of the recent sociology of religion are, on the whole, extremely narrow'.[33] It is certainly interesting that Wilson can dismiss such extra-ecclesiastical evidence as that provided by the mass media with the simple observation that, 'in spite of the evidence of large numbers who claim to listen to religious broadcasts, we cannot be at all sure that their level of attention is the same as that which prevails in church'.[34]

The consequences of Wilson's somewhat limited approach become only too obvious if one considers, for example, the role of ritual within the West. In an important sociological analysis of ritual within contemporary industrial society Robert Bocock suggests that it is still important even if largely ignored by sociologists—both within the family and within the community at large. He concludes that, 'the fact that ritual action still continues in modern industrial society is an important fact in itself, but is only a surprising one to those whose model of man underplays the importance of the non-rational elements in human beings'.[35]

It is important to note in this context that in his most recent writings Berger himself has come to doubt his thoroughgoing secularisation model. Whilst still believing that there has indeed been a process of secularisation, he now admits that he may have over-stated its power and irreversibility. Phenomena of 'religious revival' within America—presumably not all related to the institutional churches—have convinced him that there may today be a 'counter-secularisation' process evident.[36]

In addition, Berger now sets the process of secularisation within the wider context of modernisation. The latter he sees as a direct consequence of modern technology, or, more accurately, as 'the institutional concomitants of technologically induced economic growth'.[37] At the level of consciousness the phenomenon of modernisation gives rise to pluralisation, and the latter in turn gives rise to secularisation. He now follows Luckmann[38] more closely in arguing that the most visible consequence of this pattern is the 'privatisation of religion'—thus, 'while religion has had to "evacuate" one area after another in the public sphere, it has successfully maintained itself as an expression of private meaning'.[39] It is interesting to note that this thesis stands in stark contrast to that of Talcott Parsons. The latter, too, interprets the effects of 'modernism' in terms of both 'religious pluralism' and the 'privatisation of religion', but he disagrees with an interpretation of these phenomena as features of a process of secularisation. On the contrary, he argues that they can be interpreted in terms of a 'Christianising' of secular society—a process that stems at least from the Reformation.[40] Berger does, however, concede that modernisation may not be 'inexorable or inevitable'[41] itself a significant concession that Wilson has yet to make.

However Wilson's characterisation of secularisation is ultimately assessed, it is perhaps his novel interpretations of denominationalism and ecumenism that are his most important contributions to the debate. It is here that he advances in effect an *a priori* argument from structural changes in religious institutions to popular attitudes and beliefs. Since empirical data for the latter are largely non-existent, his argument represents an important attempt to probe history.

Wilson sees denominationalism as itself a manifestation of the process of secularisation in two main ways. In the first place, like Berger, he argues that the Reformation carried within it the seeds of secularisation in its 'demystification 'of the world:

> The Reformation reduced the mystical elements in religion, and Calvinism took this process further. The development of Arianism, Socinianism and Unitarianism in the eighteenth century led to a more fully rationalised religious ethic. The divinity of Christ, the miracles and the Virgin Birth all successively became open to challenge within the context of religious discussion. Tradition still had its strength, of course,

but as the influence of superstition waned, so these beliefs—even where they were still strongly held—became socially less significant.[42]

Ironically, Wilson argues that 'considering Christianity's attempt to eliminate magic, alien beliefs and rival theories of deity, religiosity as such is stronger where such multiplicity of ideas prevails—as in Hinduism'.[43] Thus in Berger's terms, the 'radical truncation' of the sacred cosmos, which took place at the Reformation, is itself part of the process of secularisation, in the sense that it directly contributes to a decline in religious belief.

This part of Wilson's understanding of denominationalism is, of course, open to the same criticisms as those facing Berger, even though the former does not extend his analysis of secularisation back into Judaism. He is forced into generalisations about the effects of the Reformation which may do justice to neither Reformation theologians nor their popular supporters. It is always possible to interpret the Reformation as part of a 'de-secularising' process,[44] by means of which the radical transcendence of Christian belief was emphasised over against the anthropomorphising tendencies of Medieval Catholicism. Such a counter-interpretation is just as possible as that of Berger and Wilson, and serves to show, at the very least, that sweeping historical generalisations of this sort are dangerous. In addition, it is always possible that, even if Reformation theology is to be interpreted in terms of the secularisation model, 'magic' and 'mystery' persisted in the beliefs of the popular supporters of the Reformation.

A further point, however, might be made. Wilson appears to have a rather monolithic understanding of religiosity in Medieval Catholicism. Implicit in his notion that the Reformation represents the beginning of a process of decline in religiosity, is an assumption that religiosity was relatively strong in pre-Reformation Catholicism. So, the Medieval Catholic Church replicated within itself the feudal society within which it was situated. This assumption may rest on the dubious equation of religiosity with religious belief, ignoring the crucial category of religious commitment. If the latter is to be included within an adequate understanding of religiosity, then it is by no means clear, even at the popular level, that religiosity was strong in Medieval Catholicism.

The very presence of monasticism within Medieval Catholicism may be an indication of a mixed level of religiosity. In his analysis of the religious order within the nineteenth century, Michael Hill argues that religious virtuosi act out a role of 'revolution by tradition':

> Virtuosi take as their central point of reference a period in the early history of their religion which can be seen as particularly authentic. They then compare this pristine model with their perception of the contemporary reality, and are impressed with the extent to which this comparison indicates a *decline*. Their response is to practise a style of religious observance which aims at *reinstating* the valued tradition.[45]

The religious virtuoso is quite different from religious charismatic figures, such as the leaders of the Reformation. The latter are more radical than the former, since they are more concerned to break away from existing religious traditions rather than abstract 'pure religion' from them. It is precisely because the religious virtuoso stands firmly within the religious tradition of his day, and yet judges it to be in decline, that his presence within any particular age suggests a mixed level of religiosity. Thus, in Medieval Catholicism, the very presence of religious orders suggests the possibility that the general level of religiosity in the population at large may not have been very high. In an age of high religiosity the religious virtuoso is presumably redundant.

No more than a possibility is suggested by this argument. However, it does at least serve to question too easy assumptions about the level of religiosity in Medieval Catholicism. It is significant that Berger and Wilson's analyses do rest on just such an assumption.

The second part to Wilson's analysis of denominationalism as a manifestation of secularisation uses the *a priori* argument from structures to beliefs, and is, perhaps, the stronger of the two parts:

> Denominational diversity, however, has in itself promoted a process of secularisation, in providing for the uncommitted a

diversity of religious choice, in creating institutionalised expression of social differences and divisions, and in the very circumstance which, in extending choice, allows some to make no choice at all. The divergence of belief systems and of ethical codes in society, short of creating a persistent state of tension, is likely to reduce the effectiveness of the religious agencies of social control. . . . The man who chooses to avoid religion altogether can now also escape religious regulation of his social life in a way not previously possible. In this sense he accepts, and the mixed religious circumstance facilitates, the growth of a secular ethic in which some basis of social control other than religious sanction—has to be developed.[46]

From transformed ecclesiastical structures, then, Wilson produces a strong *a priori* argument to the effect that the individual within a denominational society is freed to be religiously uncommitted in a way that is not so possible in a feudal society. On this understanding it is no accident that the Roman Catholic Church traditionally opposed religious libertarianism. As recently as 1885 Pope Leo XII wrote that 'the equal toleration of all religions . . . is the same thing as atheism. . . . The Church deems it unlawful to place all the religions on the same footing as the true religion'.[47] Nor is it an accident that the same Church has been traditionally, at least, suspicious of ecumenism. Religious 'tolerance' too easily becomes religious 'indifference'. This is an important view, though not one without difficulties, to which I will return later.

Wilson's analysis of ecumenism as a manifestation, not of religious strength, but of secularisation, has been examined elsewhere[48] and need not be described at length here. Briefly, he advances the original proposal that ecumenical activity within the churches is an indication of their increasing weakness, since, on organisational principles, 'organisations amalgamate when they are weak rather than when they are strong, since alliance means compromise and amendment of commitment'.[49] Again he employs an *a priori* argument from ecclesiastical structures to religious belief, even seeing ecumenical theology amongst the clergy as a prophet of organisational weakness. For Wilson, such theology becomes a 'new faith' at a time when theology in general is weak.

Wilson's argument shares many of the weaknesses of Berger's

100

interpretation of ecumenism in terms of a 'market analogy'[50]—
according to which churches combine to appeal to a religious
market in a situation where they are generally losing social
significance. I have argued elsewhere[51] that a case-study of the
breakdown of the Anglican/Methodist Union Scheme in 1969
does not appear to support either a 'market analogy' or an
'amalgamation' theory of ecumenism. As Wilson himself ably
shows, both the Church of England and the Methodist Church
have declined fairly rapidly during this century, so, on his own
theory of ecumenism, the Union Scheme should have been
accepted by both the Churches. The fact that it was not suggests
the possibility that more specifically theological variables were
involved in the situation (i.e. the theological issue of episcopal
ordination). It is also interesting that the highly complex
pattern of disruptions and unions within the Presbyterian
Churches in Scotland during the last two centuries[52] in no way
seems to correspond to moments of institutional strength or
weakness within these Churches.

Even if Wilson's argument for secularisation on the basis
of ecumenism cannot be supported from empirical data, his
a priori argument from the phenomenon of denominationalism
remains. In the absence of *a posteriori* evidence either support-
ing or contradicting an historical process of secularisation, this
evidence must be taken seriously. It provides the possibility, at
least, of a valid historical model for the sociologist of religion.

8

Sociological Critics of the Secularisation Model

WITHIN RECENT years the secularisation model has been increasingly criticised by sociologists themselves. Whereas in the last chapter I set out to examine the secularisation models employed by two of the most articulate sociological defenders of a thoroughgoing process of secularisation, in this chapter I intend to turn instead to the critics. The whole problem of secularisation within the sociology of religion has become increasingly complex—with arguments and counter-arguments abounding. Nevertheless, it remains a crucial area of interest to those concerned with the social context of theology. Only an adequate understanding of the sheer complexity of the problem can provide a satisfactory basis on which to interpret the context within which contemporary theology must work.

For the sake of clarity, critics of the secularisation model may divide into three, not necessarily mutually exclusive, categories. In the first place there are those sociologists, like David Martin, who see logical difficulties inherent within the secularisation model, however it is to be described. In the second place, there are those, like Larry Shiner, who argue that too many different meanings have been attached to the model by sociologists. And finally, there are those, like Andrew Greeley, who believe that models other than that of secularisation better interpret the contemporary data relating to religiosity within the West. All three categories of critic are united in their belief that 'secularisation should be erased from the sociological dictionary'.[1]

Logical Objections to the Secularisation Model

David Martin's paper 'Towards eliminating the concept of secularisation'[2] is, perhaps, the most celebrated critique of the secularisation model. However, the fact that this paper is often quoted but seldom criticised justifies examination of it. Martin

102

introduces at least five criticisms of the model, some of which he expands elsewhere. These criticisms may be set out formally as follows:

Secularisation models tend to . . .
(1) distinguish simplistically between 'religious' and 'secular'
(2) distinguish between 'real' and 'bogus' religiousness.
(3) be ideologically based
(4) be unhistorical in their treatment of decline
(5) ignore other possible explanations of the empirical data.

Martin makes these criticisms without referring directly to any particular sociologist who employs a secularisation model. Instead they are presented as logical difficulties that presumably confront any secularisation theorist, and, in the light of which, *any* secularisation model must be abandoned. This point is clearly implicit in the following quotation:

> The vastly varied religious situation needs to be studied apart from the pressure to illustrate a philosophical position. Values doubtless intrude into every sociological formulation, but the more egregious versions of ideological distortion can be avoided. The word secularisation is too closely linked to such distortions to be retained. Its very use encourages us to avoid studies of the impact of, for example, geographic and social mobility on religious practice, in favour of cloudy generalisations.[3]

The particular forms of 'ideological distortion' that Martin examines are rationalism, Marxism and existentialism. He does not claim that *every* secularisation theorist must be a rationalist, a Marxist or an existentialist, nor does he claim that the sociologist can ever be 'value-free', but he does claim that the word 'secularisation' is too closely linked to such 'distortion' to be useful to the sociologist. This is an argument about principles. Martin would apparently not be persuaded by Berger's frank admission that the secularisation model is sometimes 'distorted' in this way and his subsequent claim that nevertheless it is possible 'to describe the empirical phenomenon without taking up an evaluative stance'.[4] Nor would he necessarily be persuaded by Berger's obvious knowledge of the impact of 'geographic and social mobility on religious practice'.[5] Instead, he would presumably argue in principle that even Berger's carefully defined concept of secularisation encourages 'distorted'

103

ideological interpretations (criticism 3) which serve to obscure other possible explanations of contemporary religiosity (criticism 5).

The weakness of Martin's argument can again be shown in relation to his claim that secularisation models tend to be unhistorical (criticism 4). Elsewhere he claims that 'sociologists avoid the complexity of history by organising it in contrasting pairs'.[6] He presents the 'contrasting pair' offered by the secularisation theorist in a highly stylised form:

> Once upon a time the Church dominated society as the cathedral of St Hugh dominates Lincoln. The Church presented a massive, articulated, over-arching system of belief which defined the horizon of hope, here and hereafter, just as it cast the shadows of fear. The Catholic faith hallowed birth, marriage and death and dispensed social as well as eternal salvation. All thought was cast in a religious key and the texture of life woven throughout with the story of salvation. . . . Then, as the story goes, men gradually recovered the spirit of free enquiry and personal choice. The single perspective on the world was first broken in two by the Reformation and then almost immediately splintered into innumerable fragments as a growingly differentiated society spawned a comparable differentiation of viewpoint. Nowadays it is Everyman his own theologian; and if Everyman seeks legitimacy for his social arrangements or for his revolutions he is more likely to appeal to the will of the people than to the will of God.[7]

This stylised account is clearly a caricature. I suggested in the previous chapter that there are indeed parts of both Berger's and Wilson's accounts of the process of secularisation which correspond fairly closely to it. Nevertheless, there are at least two important aspects ot their argument which cannot be caricatured in this way—namely socio-structural secularisation and cultural secularization deduced from *a priori* assumptions about changing social structures. It is inadequate simply to label these two aspects of their analysis as 'unhistorical', and to dismiss them on a theory of 'contrasting pairs'. Again, the fact that *some* parts of secularisation theory tend to be 'unhistorical' does not mean that *all* parts of secularisation theory are 'unhistorical'.

It is possible that Martin's first two criticisms—namely, that secularisation models tend both to distinguish simplistically between the 'religious' and the 'secular' and to make a spurious distinction between 'real' and 'bogus' religiousness, is more firmly based. I have already argued, again in the context of Berger and Wilson, that they do have a tendency to interpret evidence of both decline in church-going in Britain and apparent increase, or at least persistence, in the States, as evidence of a process of secularisation. Such interpretations are presumably based on the assumption, despite suggestions of apparent vitality,[8] that religious organisations in the States are epiphenomenal—or, in Martin's terms, 'bogus'. Again, it is not necessary for secularisation theorists, perhaps, to make such claims, but there is a temptation to do so in the face of seemingly contradictory patterns of religious practice in the West.

Clearly, however, secularisation theorists *do* have to distinguish between the 'religious' and the 'secular', since even a minimum definition of the secularisation model claims that a society which was once comparatively 'religious' is now comparatively 'secular'. Martin has no difficulty in showing that such a distinction is difficult to achieve. Employing the Weberian distinction between 'this worldliness' and 'other worldliness', he shows that the latter can refer either to a belief in after-life or to a mystical state achieved within the world as now constituted. He contends that 'both interpretations of other worldliness are legitimate and are far from being mutually exclusive'.[9] The effect of this observation is to create a quandary:

> Even a short survey of the apparently simple distinction between this and other worldliness discloses something of the range of criteria available. It may be confidently anticipated that parallel complications arise in relation to the other contrasts . . . between mythopoeic and factual, conditional and ineluctable, and so on. Broadly, there are two ways of dealing with the difficulties posed by the existence of such variety. Either one can attempt to *link* the polar extremes of the various continua in such a way that one set of poles defines religion while the other set defines secularity. Or one can *select* one dichotomy as furnishing the crucial contrast between the religious and the secular.[10]

He argues that there is no association 'in logic or in practice between any one pole and any grouping of the others'.[11] In addition, he argues that the second method is too 'expensive', since it leads to 'unintelligibility' when interpreting actual religious data. The empirical situation is more complex than simple contrasts between 'this worldly' and 'other worldly', or 'religious' and 'secular', allow. Nor does Martin believe that conventional definitions of 'religion' in terms of institutional religion avoid this problem, since the secularisation theorist is obliged to specify the common characteristics of 'religious' institutions, and presumably distinguish them from 'secular' institutions.

Martin's argument is important but not totally convincing. Undoubtedly some secularisation theorists do make a simplistic distinction between the 'religious' and the 'secular', but *every* sociologist of religion, whether he is a secularisation theorist or not, is obliged to offer a definition of religion at some point. He may simply regard his definition as a heuristic device, but he can make little sense of his subject if he does not have such a device.

Others too[12] have recognised that the secularisation model is dependent on a definition of 'religion', and that the type of definition adopted will affect the types of empirical data that are relevant to the model. So, for example, a functionalist/inclusive type of definition (i.e. based on what religion 'does') may well render it difficult to maintain a secularisation model at all, whereas a substantive/exclusive type of definition (i.e. based on what religion 'is') allows a number of possible secularisation models. This point can be demonstrated quite simply.

In Chapter 1 I argued that Yinger's functionalist/inclusive definition of religion is problematic. Whether one defines religion with Yinger as 'a system of beliefs and practices by means of which a group of people struggles with the ultimate problems of human life',[13] or whether with John Bowker as 'route-finding activities, homeostatic and conservative, focused on particular compounds of limitation',[14] almost any form of ideology could be viewed as 'religious'. On this argument almost any type of secularisation model becomes impossible *by definition*. It might be possible to show, for example, that Christianity and Christian belief were declining in the West, but that of itself would not demonstrate a process of secularisation. Instead, such a demonstration might open up the possibility that Christianity was simply being replaced by another form of ideology. It is difficult even to conceive of a society which is not in some sense concerned with 'ultimate problems' or 'compounds of limitation'. Consequently it is not surprising to discover that Yinger himself resists the notions of secularisation or even religious decline, and argues instead for social change.[15] By definition he is obliged to argue in this way.

However, there is in fact an implicit substantive element in both Yinger's and Bowker's apparently functionalist definition. Neither writer is content to identify *any* 'ultimate problem' or 'compound of limitation' as 'religious'. Durkheim's classic definition of religion has often been criticised for the same reason.[16] Thus, when he defined religion as 'a unified system of beliefs and practices relative to sacred things, that is to say, things set apart and forbidden—beliefs and practices which unite into a single moral community called a church all those who adhere to them',[17] he gave no further definition of 'sacred things'. It is quite clear that Durkheim did not mean *anything* 'set apart and forbidden', however trivial.

Substantive/exclusive definitions do at least allow for the possibility of a secularisation model, since they usually do specify some substantive item within society which can decline. So, for example, Tylor's minimum definition of religion as 'a belief in spiritual beings',[18] makes a secularisation model at least possible. If it could be demonstrated that 'a belief in spiritual beings' was declining in contemporary industrialised society, then the term secularisation might be justified. The weakness of Tylor's particular definition, of course, is that it seems to exclude movements which are usually classified as 'religious', such as Buddhism.

Roland Robertson offers a more sophisticated version of the substantive/exclusive type of definition. He provides a two-part definition of 'religious culture' as follows:

> Religious culture is that set of beliefs and symbols (and values deriving directly therefrom) pertaining to a distinction between an empirical and a super-empirical, transcendent reality; the affairs of the empirical being subordinated in significance to the non-empirical.[19]

Inevitably there are weaknesses in this definition as well. So,

107

it apparently ignores the possibility that some traditional cultures, notably in parts of Africa and New Guinea, do not distinguish between the 'empirical' and the 'non-empirical'. Nevertheless, it does exclude phenomena such as 'flag-waving', which are not usually construed as 'religious', but which tend to be included within the net of functionalist definitions. Interestingly, Robertson's definition does include such phenomena as 'magic' and 'astrology', especially when these are taken seriously within a particular culture. Robertson rightly recognises that his definition allows for the possibility of a secularisation model,[20] since it is in principle possible to show whether or not people within the West do in fact distinguish between the 'empirical' and the 'non-empirical', and if they do whether or not they tend to subordinate the affairs of the 'empirical' to the affairs of the 'non-empirical'.

Whatever the difficulties in providing an adequate definition of religion, it is no criticism of secularisation models to suggest that they are dependent on these varying definitions. The whole of the sociology of religion is so dependent—and it can afford neither to ignore problems of definition[21] nor to capitulate in the face of them.

This quandary finds parallels in other fields of sociology. Concepts such as 'class', 'status' and 'power' are widely used in sociology and yet receive no unequivocal definition. Some would doubtless maintain that the very ambiguity of these concepts renders them unsuitable for the scientific examination of society. Most sociologists, however, would probably not agree—for them the concepts of 'class', 'status' and 'power' remain useful despite their ambiguity. For such sociologists it remains incumbent on them to provide their own definition of these concepts.

Within the sociology of race relations there are undoubtedly some theorists who argue that the concept of 'race relations' should be abandoned in favour of something else—such as stratification theory. The sociologist John Rex, however, disagrees with these reductionists, arguing instead for a theoretical definition of a race relations situation.[22] However adequate or otherwise his definition may be within the context of race relations, his general argument is illuminating in the present context. Rex is determined to argue, not just against the reductionists, but also against the empiricists within race relations who are disinterested in problems of definition. Against the latter, in particular, he claims that some of the main empirical studies of race relations within Britain and the States have been misdirected because of insufficient attention to the problem of definition.

Semantic Objections to the Secularisation Model

This general point about the ambiguity contained in many key sociological concepts leads naturally to the second category of sociological critic of the secularisation model. Larry Shiner and others[23] have attempted to set out the various meanings that have been attached to the term 'secularisation'. Shiner proposes the following five 'ideal types'[24]:

Secularisation is conceived as . . .

(1) the decline of religion
(2) conformity with the world
(3) the desacralisation of the world
(4) the disengagement of society from religion
(5) the transposition of beliefs and patterns of behaviour from the 'religious' to the 'secular' sphere.

The first of these ideal types might be seen as the minimum definition of the secularisation model—i.e. religious decline. In a sense the other four ideal types are aspects of religious decline, since they all represent a historical process—a process probably disadvantageous to religion. Shiner identifies this type as representing a process by which 'the religious doctrines, values, and institutions which once dominated or informed the society lose their status and influence'.[25] Like Martin, he believes that the ambiguous empirical and historical data connected with religious phenomena do not support such a projected process.

Shiner identifies the second type as the process by which 'the religious group increasingly turns its attention from the supernatural and the next life and becomes more and more preoccupied with and similar to the surrounding society . . . the culmination of secularisation in this sense would be a religious group indistinguishable from society'.[26] The main difficulty with this type for Shiner lies in deciding whether or not a particular instance of apparent 'conformity with the world' really does involve the surrender of something integral to the particular religious tradition at stake. In effect does 'conformity' necessarily involve 'compromise', as Wilson suggests?

The third type Shiner identifies as the process by which 'the world is gradually deprived of its sacred character as man and nature become the object of rational-causal explanation and manipulation . . . the culmination of secularisation would be a completely "rational" world society in which the phenomenon of the supernatural or even of "mystery" would play no part'.[27] Shiner suggests that this type of secularisation is not applicable in the West since desacralisation is already apparent within both Judaism and Christianity—here the world is not understood as 'permeated with sacred powers'.[28]

The fourth type is the process by which 'society separates itself from the religious understanding which has previously informed it in order to constitute itself an autonomous reality and consequently to limit to the sphere of private life . . . the culmination of secularisation in this sense would be a religion of a purely inward character influencing neither institutions nor corporate action, and a society in which religion made no appearance outside the sphere of the religious group'.[29] As with the 'conformity with the world' type, Shiner stresses that this type of 'disengagement of society' need not be viewed in negative terms. It remains to be shown whether or not 'conformity' or 'disengagement' actually involve 'compromise' for religion.

The final type is seen as the process by which 'aspects of religious belief or experience are shifted from their sacral context to a purely human context . . . the calculation of this kind of secularisation process would be a totally anthropological religion and a society which had taken over all the functions previously attached to the religious institutions'.[30] Weber's thesis of the 'Protestant Ethic and the Spirit of Capitalism' is an obvious example of this, and Shiner suggests that it well illustrates the difficulties involved in the type. It is always extremely difficult to identify actual survivals of religious beliefs in a 'purely human' context:

Shiner's five types have proved important within the sociology of religion,[31] even though, as he admits himself, they are not necessarily mutually exclusive. So, the final three in particular are hard to distinguish at times—'desacralisation' and 'disengagement' may appear as opposite sides of the same phenomenon, and 'transposition' may be a feature of 'conformity'. Further, as noted, all may be interpreted in terms of 'religious decline'. Their cumulative effect, however, is to produce doubt about the secularisation model in Shiner's mind:

> One conclusion which might seem to be imposed by our analysis so far is that the term 'secularisation' should be dropped entirely. During its long development it has often served the partisans of religious and anti-religious controversy and has constantly taken on new meanings without completely losing the old ones. As a result it is swollen with overtones and implications, especially those associated with indifference or hostility to religion. . . . Often the same writer will use it in two or more senses without acknowledging the shift of meaning.[32]

Such a conclusion, however, does not seem to be demanded of itself from Shiner's analysis. Neither his exposition of the ambiguity of the secularisation model in terms of five ideal types, nor his individual criticism of these types, logically requires the abandonment of the model. Again, the fact that a sociological concept receives no universally agreed, unequivocal definition, does not usually entail its abandonment. Instead, it only demands that those sociologists who use it should be careful to distinguish which definition they intend to employ. Having decided upon this the sociologist must then face the particular criticisms that might be brought against his definition. Shiner concedes this final point only because he believes 'a moratorium on any widely used term is unlikely to be successful'.[33] Much more important though, is the possibility that the secularisation model might still be useful despite the ambiguities and criticisms it faces.[34]

One final point should be made in this context. It is possible that Shiner's five ideal types serve in the end to obscure the full range of ambiguity involved in the secularisation model. In terms of the analysis made in previous chapters a far more complex picture emerges. On a minimum definition of secularisation in terms of 'religious decline', the following choices must be made by the sociologist, since both terms 'religious' and 'decline' are themselves ambiguous:

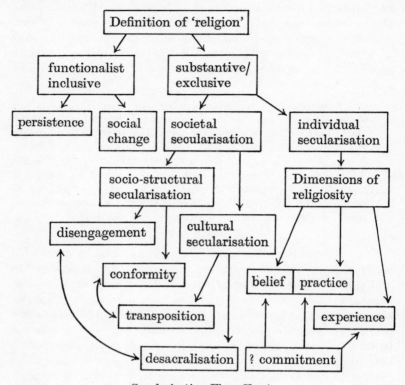

Secularisation Flow-Chart

Again, the fact that the sociologist must make these choices does not thereby invalidate the secularisation model. It merely means that he should be aware of the choices he makes. Doubtless, even this chart is not exhaustive on a minimum definition of 'religious decline', but it does at least serve to show that the secularisation model is considerably more complex than that allowed by Shiner's five ideal types.

Alternative Models to Secularisation

The final category of sociological critics of the secularisation model concerns those who hold that models other than that of secularisation better interpret the contemporary data relating to religiosity within the West. It has already been noted that one of Martin's criticisms (5) of the secularisation model is that it tends to ignore other possible explanations of the empirical data. However, this criticism should be distinguished from Andrew Greeley's more thoroughgoing attempt to substitute a model of 'persistence' for that of secularisation. Martin's approach is far more *ad hoc* and less sweeping than that of Greeley.

Martin's alternative explanations are modest. So, for example, when confronted with the obvious evidence of decline in church-going in Britain, Martin suggests an alternative to the explanation offered by a secularisation model:

> Of course, fewer people in our contemporary society go to church than in Victorian Britain, however you estimate the piety of that time. Yet this does not in any way lend itself to a simple linear explanation of trends. Dr Yeo's remarkable work[35] on the local history of religion suggests that the decline in the activity of religious institutions is exactly parallel to the decline of participation in all voluntary associations whether religious *or* secular. Those voluntary associations concerned with religion may have stood up against very general tendencies in our society somewhat better than most.[36]

This explanation is certainly interesting, and produces a counter-balance to easy assumptions about cultural secularisation—in terms of which decline in religious practice might be interpreted as a result of the spread of an increasingly 'rational' world-view. Nevertheless, it may not be very effective in countering other types of secularisation theory. So, for example, Wilson's view that religious institutions are becoming increasingly epiphenomenal would seem to be confirmed by the observation that decline in church-going is related to decline in attendance at all voluntary associations. Religious institutions are thereby in effect equated with voluntary associations, and attendance at the one is viewed as equally epiphenomenal as attendance at the other.

In principle, though, Martin is performing an important function in suggesting alternative models to explain the exigencies of contemporary data for religious phenomena. Only in this way can the secularisation model be seriously tested.

Greeley, however, is not simply concerned to suggest *ad hoc* explanations of religious phenomena to counter the secularisation model. Instead he sets out to replace the secularisation model with the model of the 'persistence of religion'. In contrast to secularisation theorists, Greeley argues that 'however much the context has changed, the basic functions religion plays in human life are essentially the same'[37] as they always have been throughout human history. To support this massive claim, Greeley suggests the following five ways in which the function of religion has remained constant:[38]

Religion provides man with . . .

(1) a meaning system to cope with the question of the Ultimate
(2) a feeling of belonging with a communal group sharing the same ultimate commitments (*gemeinschaft*)
(3) a means of integrating life with the forces of human sexuality
(4) a channel for coming into intimate contact with the sacred
(5) leaders whose role is to provide comfort and challenge when man attempts to wrestle with the Ultimate.

In advancing his persistence model, however, he does not deny that there have been certain changes in religion. So, he admits that 'religion has no direct influence over the large corporate structures which have emerged in the last four hundred years. Big Government, Big Business, Big Labour, Big Military and Big Education are not directly influenced either by religion or by church'.[39] In effect this admission concedes something close to a disengagement theory of socio-structural secularisation, if not a desacralisation theory. This impression seems to be confirmed by his subsequent admissions that 'a considerable number of phenomena which once received a directly religious interpretation now can be explained by rational science', that man today tends to think in abstract thought rather than myths, and that 'religion is a more explicit and individual matter now than it has ever been in the past',[40] with the individual having a greater freedom of choice relating to religious commitment. For Greeley, however, all these changes simply concern the context and not the functions of religion—the latter remain unchanged.

It becomes clear that the main object of Greeley's attack is the evolutionary assumptions that he sees implicit in the secularisation model. In concluding his examination of these assumptions he argues:

> We have argued that the conventional wisdom about contemporary religion is inadequate to explain vast amounts of empirical data, and we have found that this inadequacy is based on doctrinaire and *a priori* assumptions about the nature of human social change. These assumptions imply a simple-minded, unidirectional, organic evolutionary model which was initially merely descriptive but quite quickly became normative: not only has religion declined, not only is it in crisis, but the decline and the crisis are things that *ought* to be because they represent a triumph of enlightenment and rationality over the obscurantism, ignorance and superstition of the past.[41]

It is possible that Greeley, like Martin, claims too much. Certain secularisation theories may indeed be based on a 'simplified, unidirectional, organic, evolutionary model', of a prescriptive rather than descriptive nature,[42] but that is not to show that *all* secularisation theories are so based. Clearly, Berger does not hail the process of secularisation as a 'triumph of enlightenment', nor does he appear to set the process within an evolutionary context.

Greeley believes that theories of secularisation presuppose that society is evolving from *gemeinschaft* to *gesellschaft*—that is, from communal relationships to associational relationships. Against this presupposition he argues that 'the basic ties of friendship, primary relationship, land, faith, common origin and consciousness of kind persist much as they did in the Ice Age . . . they are the very stuff out of which society is made, and in their absence the corporate structures would collapse'.[43] Instead of a direct evolution from *gemeinschaft* to *gesellschaft*, he suggests that there has been 'a tremendous complexification of society, with vast pyramids of corporate structures being erected on a substratum of primordial relationships'.[44] Within this second situation Greeley believes that a persistence model of religion can gain credence. The functions of religion persist because the *gemeinschaft* infrastructure of society also persists, albeit in a more complex social situation today than in the past.

Greeley's critique of evolutionary social assumptions is important. Although few social theorists today would propose the overtly evolutionary theories of society offered in the nineteenth century,[45] evolutionary-type assumptions nevertheless do persist, even within the sociology of religion.[46]

John Bowker's analysis of religion in terms of 'homeostatic' and 'conservative' route-finding activities provides an interesting example of this tendency. He argues that man, like all organisms, is set within the context of compounds of limitation, to which he must adapt, for otherwise he will not survive (conservatism), and from which he seeks to escape (homeostatic—or the state of goal-seeking). The compounds of limitation of the Devonian lung-fish, for example, were originally aquatic and only subsequently terrestrial. Just because this fish already had lungs and limbs it was able to survive the new compounds of limitation presented by land when droughts came. The combined effects of homeostasis and conservatism ensured that the lung-fish both survived drought and emerged as a new form of life. Similarly, self-conscious man is able to overcome his particular compounds of limitation, death and time, through his culture and scientific achievements. Man shares with the ape his evolutionary context: 'the ape and the pianist have in common, both with each other and with all life an evolutionary context, an ability to find a way through the compounds of limitation which threaten the continuity of their existence: either that, or they perish.'[47]

It is important to recognise, though, that the theory of evolution is nothing at all to do with social development, but is rather a retrospective hypothesis of physical *change*. A theory of 'development' as such clearly involves value-judgements, as Bowker himself admits;[48] it is by no means obvious that such concepts as 'self-consciousness' and 'complexity' in themselves denote 'development'—their opposites might equally denote 'development'.

Even if one eliminates notions of 'development' from evolutionary social assumptions, it is still not clear that evolution is relevant to religious phenomena. The hypothesis of physical evolution takes seriously the notion of the 'survival of the fittest', but, unless one is to adopt a Durkheimian theory of some form of religion being essential for the survival of a

116

society, religion would appear to be exluded from such a notion. There is, in addition, a certain strangeness in applying evolutionary assumptions to either religion in particular or society in general. Such assumptions in science refer to periods of some millions of years, whereas, in the context of religion or society, they often refer to comparatively short spans of time.

Nevertheless, it remains to be shown that there is a necessary relationship between societal models of evolution and the secularisation model—or, indeed, that the latter necessarily presupposes an evolution from *gemeinschaft* to *gesellschaft*. No necessary relationship between these models in fact exists. Rather their common factor seems to be the use of sweeping historical models—and it is just at this point that Greeley's own model of persistence is most open to criticism.

Undoubtedly the model of persistence is an important counter-balance to thoroughgoing secularisation models. Yet it shares with such models a preparedness to apply a single model to a considerable span of history, even when the empirical data is often weak or absent. At the most superficial level it is obviously true that religion has persisted throughout recorded history. However, Greeley's claims clearly seek to go beyond this platitude, since no secularisation theorist would be prepared to deny it. Instead, he argues that society is essentially conservative, and that the actual functions of religion have remained unchanged throughout history. Even evidence of apparent disengagement of society from religion does not dissuade him from this claim. He can only achieve consistency at this point by distinguishing between the 'context' and 'function' of religion, and by ascribing disengagement to the former and not to the latter.

The validity of the sweeping historical model is clearly crucial to the secularisation debate. It appears that the advocates of a persistence model of religion are as dependent upon it as the supporters of a thoroughgoing secularisation model. This point has fundamental relevance to the social context of theology, and must be pursued in the next and final chapter.

One important point, however, emerges from both this chapter and the last. Neither the proponents of a thoroughgoing secularisation model nor the critics of any secularisation model are entirely persuasive. Weaknesses and ambiguities face

117

sociologists of either persuasion. As yet, it would appear, the secularisation debate which has dominated much of the sociology of religion over the last decade has not been conclusively settled. Secularisation remains a live issue.

9

Towards a New Model

THE AIM of this book has been to explore just one of at least
three possible interactions between theology and sociology—
that of the social context of theology. A small amount of scholarship has been devoted to the approach which attempts to test
the hypothesis that theology and theological ideas may at times
act as independent variables, both within society as a whole
and amongst sociologists in particular. Considering the importance that Weber placed on this hypothesis it may indeed seem
strange that so little sociological research has actually used this
approach. Even less scholarship has been devoted to the
approach which seeks to explore the social determinants of
particular theological positions. There is a small, but growing,
amount of interest amongst sociologists in the social determinants of moral ideas—though even here this has traditionally
been a pursuit of anthropologists rather than sociologists. The
social determinants of theological positions remains a comparatively neglected area of academic interest. However, the
most neglected of the three approaches is probably the third.
Although its importance might appear as somewhat marginal
to sociologists, I have argued that it is of central importance to
the theologian.

In exploring the social context of theology, I have argued
that contemporary theologians both do and ought to make
assumptions about this context. Chapters 4 and 6 attempted to
show some of the societal assumptions that recent theologians
have in fact made. It is clear, even on the most superficial
sociological analysis, that these assumptions are seldom substantiated in any satisfactory way. So, in the first of these
chapters I sought to show that the societal assumptions made
by Harvey Cox and John Robinson do not stand up to any sort
of sociological scrutiny. In the second of the chapters I concentrated on one specific area——assumptions that theologians

tend to make about the secularisation model. I argued that this model is likely to continue to be important within both theological and sociological circles. Again, it was apparent that the assumptions which theologians tend to make about secularisation are often remarkably unsophisticated.

Despite the fact that theologians frequently appear to be 'amateur sociologists', making claims about society which defy sociological analysis and ignoring the work of sociologists of religion themselves, I have also argued that they should indeed be concerned with the social context within which they work. Employing the notion of plausibility structures, drawn from the sociology of knowledge, I argued that the theologian cannot afford to ignore societal plausibility structures. An adequate appreciation of communication seems to demand that the communicator should at least take seriously the plausibility structures of those with whom he is attempting to communicate. The theologian, it has been argued, is subject to the same canons.

Hopefully, however, the theologian will increasingly be concerned to study the work of sociologists, in an effort to equip himself with substantiable societal assumptions. It is with this aim in mind that I have devoted the last two chapters to the specifically sociological debate about the secularisation model. The first of these chapters attempted to analyse the thoroughgoing secularisation models of Berger and Wilson, whereas the second concentrated on the sociological critics of the model, notably Martin, Shiner and Greeley. So much space devoted to a single model needs little justification in view of its sheer complexity and of its centrality in the recent writings of both sociologists of religion and theologians. Of course it is not the only model through which to interpret the social context of theology, but it is perhaps the most crucial.

No matter how many other possible models might have been employed to explore the social context of theology, the object of the present analysis is methodological rather than substantive. That is, the aim of this book has not been to explore every single possible model that might be relevant to the social context of theology, even if that were possible. Instead, its aim is simply to justify the claim that social context is relevant to theology and to suggest ways in which this relevance might be better pursued. In exploring the secularisation model, then, I am not making any exclusive claims about it. Other models would indeed be possible and relevant. However, by focusing upon a single model my implicit methodology should be becoming more explicit. It will be the object of this chapter to attempt to uncover this methodology further.

Ambiguities in the Secularisation Debate

It will be evident that there are weaknesses in the arguments presented both by defenders and critics of a secularisation model. I have suggested in the context of advocates of a thoroughgoing secularisation model that it is only cultural and socio-structural models that avoid the criticisms of the sociological critics. In the context of the critics I have suggested that the secularisation model is not necessarily undermined by Martin's logical objections, Shiner's semantic objections or Greeley's model of persistence. However, it remains to re-examine the adequacy of cultural and socio-structural models.

The argument I tentatively accepted for a cultural model was based on an *a priori* case. This argument recognises that *a posteriori* historical evidence for cultural secularisation is frankly weak. Nevertheless, it suggests that there is a relationship between societal structures and popular beliefs. Accordingly, the popular culture that exists within a pluralist society must be very different from that which exists within a more traditional society. One would certainly expect a more monochrome world-view in the latter than in the former. Today, it is suggested, we live in a situation of social pluralism and ecclesiastical denominationalism, so our religious beliefs will inevitably be less unified than those of a traditional society. It is tempting to conclude that the logical outcome of this *a priori* argument is the desacralisation model of secularisation. The effect of contemporary pluralism and denominationalism is to undermine the 'sacred cosmos' of society at large.

It is clear that this *a priori* argument is based on the belief that we do in fact live in an increasingly pluralist society. David Martin, in fact, denies this assumption:

> We live, some sociologists suggest, in a pluralistic society in which all views are relativised by competition. Curiously enough, I would argue that our religion is less pluralistic than

it was in Victorian times. Enclaves of Hindus and Muslims and enclaves of middle class humanists do not in themselves necessarily make Britain a religiously pluralistic society. In fact, the religion of modern Britain is a deistic, moralistic religion-in-general, which combines a fairly high practice of personal prayer with a considerable degree of superstition.[1]

Interestingly, Martin's argument might be supported by Bryan Wilson's own study of sects. It must seem strange that sectarianism can still flourish in an apparently pluralist society, that is in a society, in Wilson's own words, in which men 'assess the world in empirical and rational terms'.[2] Yet it is quite clear that sectarian, strongly-held beliefs do persist in contemporary Western society. However, in his original study of sects,[3] Wilson suggested the mechanisms by which they maintain these strong beliefs from one generation to another—no matter how much these beliefs are at variance with those of the rest of society. Notably in the way sects construct their social life, they are able to remain as enclaves within an apparently pluralist, denominational society.

An obvious objection to this argument is that sects only represent a very small minority of the population in industrialised societies. So, it would still be possible to maintain that the majority of people are indeed influenced by pluralism and denominationalism. This argument, though, ignores the fact that the sort of social mechanisms Wilson identified in the context of sects are to be found, in part at least, within larger religious institutions. The Roman Catholic Church represents an obvious example, with its system of educational facilities. Further, most religious institutions attempt to provide at least some social facilities for their younger members. Religious socialisation is an important feature of most religious institutions,[4] and may be under-estimated at times as the means by which religious beliefs are maintained despite societal pressures.

However, even if it is true that Western society is more pluralist than it was in the past, and that this pluralism has a direct cultural effect, it is still not entirely clear that this effect will be desacralisation. This assumption is made too readily. I suggested in the previous chapter that either desacralisation or transposition might result from cultural secularisation. Thus it is by no means certain that specifically religious beliefs and values disappear even within a situation of cultural pluralism.[5]

More crucially, though, it is again not clear that the effects of pluralism must be interpreted in terms of a secularisation model at all. Andrew Greeley interprets these effects quite differently when he admits the following as one of the changes that have taken place today in the West:

> Religious commitment is, at least to some extent, a matter of free choice. Within social, cultural, and linguistic contexts a man may be able to play the role of a consumer in the super-market of religions. Even if most men do not in fact exercise the option of choosing a religion very different from that which they inherited, they are at least aware of the possibility of choice. . . . With the possibility of option there comes the immense burden of decision, but the need to *decide* about religion makes religion a more central and explicit question than it has ever been before. Insofar as an ever-increasing number of people must, in some fashion or the other, face the religious issues as explicit and central, it is legitimate, I think, to argue that the present era is *more religious* than any one of the past.[6]

Greeley's argument is important, not because it is necessarily right, but because it well illustrates the thesis that evidence of apparent secularisation can equally be interpreted as evidence of de-secularisation. It has already been noted that thorough-going secularisation theorists such as Berger or Wilson do tend to interpret seemingly contradictory evidence—such as divergent patterns of church-going—as evidence of secularisation. They might equally have interpreted such evidence as evidence of de-secularisation. Thus, in the single case of church-going, the comparatively high level of church-going in the States might be treated by sociologists as the norm, and the comparatively high level of church-non-attendance in Britain as the epiphenomenon. Both pieces of evidence might in this way appear as evidence of de-secularisation.

Yinger, of course, would see these conflicting interpretations of church-going as simply the product of wrong definitions of religion.[7] Given his own functionalist/inclusive definition of religion it is difficult to identify any change in church-going as

123

such as a product of either secularisation or de-secularisation. His argument, though becomes particularly crucial in the context of religious belief:

> If one defines religion statically—in terms of a system of beliefs and practices that emerged at a given time and were subject thereafter to no *essential* revision—religious change is nearly identical with secularisation. It represents the falling away from the great tradition. If one thinks of religion, however, as an ongoing search, subject to changed forms and revised myths, then lack of orthodoxy does not mean weakening of religion. It can be a sign of strength.[8]

The point that Yinger is making is not in fact tied to his own functionalist understanding of religion. Substantive/inclusive understandings of religion, too, can be interpreted both statically and dynamically. Again, this illustrates the thesis that evidence of apparent secularisation—in this case a decline in 'orthodox' belief—can equally be interpreted as evidence of de-secularisation.

Exactly the same thesis can be applied to socio-structural arguments for secularisation. These arguments are usually based on a shift away from ecclesiastical control that has occurred in most Western countries—a shift that is clearly still occurring in Italy and Ireland. The control that the churches once had over educational, medical and social agencies in the West has gradually been eroded. Religious functionaries once played a significant role in all three spheres, but increasingly this is no longer the case. Socio-structural arguments usually suggest that this shift has resulted in the gradual separation of Church from state, with the consequent loss of social significance of the former at the expense of the latter.

Again, it was noted in the last chapter that this socio-structural model is ambiguous. Whereas some secularisation theorists have interpreted it in terms of a disengagement model, others have interpreted it in terms of a comformity model. It is not entirely clear, then, whether religious institutions in the West are becoming increasingly separated from the state, or whether they are becoming increasingly conformed to it.

More significantly, though, it is again not certain that this shift is really evidence of a process of secularisation. In this instance, too, it is possible to argue that in fact it represents a process of de-secularisation. Interesting support for such an argument might be gleaned from the fact that religious institutions within both Britain and the States have at times themselves welcomed the adoption by the state of medical, educational and social facilities.

Michael Hill suggests a similar argument in his account of the religious order in nineteenth-century Britain. He argues that the secularisation model today suggests that 'as institutions become more and more differentiated, in the sense of occupying a more and more specific area of competence, then the church, which originally had diffuse functions, occupies a less and less significant social role'.[9] In contrast to this model, Hill suggests that it is possible that 'the process of differentiation involves the church just as it involves other institutions, and that the revival of the religious life which began in the nineteenth-century Church of England was one aspect of the adoption of the church's organisation to enable it to fulfil more effectively its specialised religious functions'.[10] Later he clarifies this concept further:

> Just as it has been argued that other institutions have taken over 'non-essential' functions of the family and have left it to provide 'core' functions, so it can be argued that religious institutions have more and more tended to fulfil specifically 'religious' functions. Whether or not this can be termed 'desecularisation' is an interesting problem.[11]

Hill leaves this point unresolved. However, he clearly believes that there is a certain ambiguity here, to which a straightforward secularisation model does less than justice. Neither does it seem that he is totally prepared to commit himself to a de-secularisation model.

This ambiguity is important because it appears at every stage of the secularisation debate. It goes beyond the sort of ambiguity expressed in the chart in the previous chapter. The latter simply sought to show that the secularisation theorist himself is faced with a number of choices in the formation of his model. Much will depend on the sort of definition of religion that he employs and on whether he is concentrating on individual religiosity or society as a whole. However, the sort of ambiguity that is encountered in the general secularisation debate is more far-reaching. It suggests the very real possibility that almost any evidence of apparent secularisation can equally be interpreted as evidence of de-secularisation.

An Alternating Model

There are, perhaps, two possible reactions to this ambiguity. The first reaction is simply to pursue a secularisation or de-secularisation model relentlessly, as if the ambiguity did not exist. By far the largest number of sociologists involved in the debate appear to adopt this approach. So, until very recently, Berger has maintained a thoroughgoing secularisation model, despite the suggestions of Luckman,[12] Bellah[13] and others that there are indications of persisting, but non-ecclesiastical, religiosity within Western society. It seems that only the emergence of recent religious youth movements, such as the 'Jesus People', has persuaded him otherwise. Conversely, Martin is content to suggest *ad hoc* alternatives to the secularisation model, without ever indicating whether or not these alternatives are intended to cover *all* the evidence used by secularisation theorists. Undoubtedly, Martin has performed a useful function in pointing to logical inconsistencies in the model propounded by some secularisation theorists, but I have argued that his logical difficulties do not cover all possible secularisation models.

The other possible reaction is to take the ambiguity seriously, and to frame the sort of model which takes it into account. Such a reaction would in effect be an admission of the complexities and vagaries of religious phenomena even within the West. It is frequently admitted that there are important respects in which exact correspondence cannot be sought between religion in industrialised societies and religion in primal societies. Some even despair of finding a definition of religion which would fit both kinds of society.[14] However, it is too easily assumed that Western religion is comparatively homogeneous and susceptible to interpretation through unified and mono-directional models such as secularisation or persistence.

I would argue that this second reaction better suits the evidence. The sheer ambiguity encountered at every stage in the secularisation debate simply ought not to be ignored. Only a model which treats it seriously can provide an adequate basis for interpreting religious phenomena in the West. Neither the contemporary nor the historical data of either individual or societal religiosity seem to conform to a linear, uniform model. Sweeping historical models in particular—whether in terms of social evolution, secularisation, persistence or whatever—appear to distort the evidence and ignore important ambiguities.

It seems possible, then, that a degree of agnosticism is essential concerning theories of any *overall* process of religious change or persistence. Too often the historical evidence is weak, and even more often the evidence is simply ambiguous. Just as few today would venture an authoritative opinion on whether or not industrialised society is actually 'developing', or even 'more developed', than primal society, so we may well have to be agnostic about the overall social status of religion in the West. Certainly the overall predictions of some of the pioneer social scientists on religion—such as Comte, Durkheim, or even Weber—have not proved particularly accurate. There is little reason to imagine that the overall predictions of contemporary social scientists will be any better.

In contrast I would suggest that the sociologist of religion has a more limited and proximate task. Instead of framing sweeping historical models, he might concentrate on more immediate models which can interpret the existing ambiguities within religious phenomena. To do this he may have to accept less literal models than he is accustomed to using. In part his task then becomes comparable to that of the scientist working at microscopic levels of reality. For example, the well known phenomenon of the wave-particle dualism of electrons, and other similar phenomena, have suggested the principle of complementarity, whereby seemingly contradictory notions are applied alternately to the same entity. As a result, models such as that of the wave-particle in science are no longer picturable in literal terms or reducible to non-analogical language. Ian Barbour, in fact, believes that 'the abandonment of picturability is one of the striking features of modern physics':[15] the atomic world, in particular, 'is not only inaccessible to direct observation, and inexpressible in terms of the senses; we are unable to even imagine it'.[16]

The parallel I am attempting to make at this point can, of course, be pushed too far. There is no need to claim that society

127

must be treated by the sociologist in the same way as micro-nature is by the physicist. Nevertheless, an obvious point of correspondence lies in the sheer ambiguity that appears to surround religious phenomena. It is possible that the principle of complementarity is relevant here. An alternating model of secularisation and dec-secularisation might provide a more adequate way of coping with this ambiguity than would a single model of either secularisation or de-secularisation. Such a model would indeed be irreducible, but it might allow the sociologist of religion 'to make new connections', in the manner which Max Black suggested was the true function of models.[17] In addition—and this is crucial—an alternating model would allow the sociologist to apply apparently contradictory explanations *to the same phenomena*. The evidence of religiosity available in the West suggests, not simply that there are some phenomena which are most adequately interpreted in terms of secularisation and other phenomena which are not, but that the same phenomena can equally be interpreted in terms of secularisation or de-secularisation.

An alternating model of secularisation and de-secularisation is essentially prosaic: it does not refer to 'historical sweeps', though it may indeed be applicable to a number of historical periods taken in isolation. So, for example, it does not necessarily support an equilibrium theory of history or society: it remains agnostic about the *overall* status of religion. Nevertheless, it does suggest that there are processes of both secularisation and de-secularisation apparent within contemporary society, and possibly within all societies. Whether or not either of these processes will finally obliterate the other must remain a matter for speculation, though at present it might seem an unlikely eventuality.

It is not possible to follow through the full ramifications of this alternating model in the present context. However, it would be irresponsible not to indicate some of the ways in which it might be used. Accordingly, just two brief examples might be taken, the first from the sphere of academic plausibility structures and the second from the sphere of popular plausibility structures.

It is not difficult to build up an argument to the effect that there has been a process of cultural secularisation apparent within the academic community for at least the last one hundred years. Such an argument might be based either on the desacralisation model or on the transposition model of secularisation. On the basis of the first it could be argued that theology, metaphysics and religious ideas in general have become increasingly epiphenomenal within the academic community. During this century alone the rise of Logical Positivism within philosophy and the accompanying positivism and behaviourism within other disciplines—such as psychology, sociology, anthropology, and linguistics—has done much to discredit the validity of religious phenomena. In a very real sense the academic community has increasingly become desacralised—a process that finds its counterpart in the socio-structural secularisation evidenced by the disengagement of theology from other academic pursuits or by its growing conformity to the dominant positivism (e.g. van Buren). On the basis of the transposition model it could also be argued that social and political scientists such as Marx, Weber, and Durkheim are the 'secular' heirs to the metaphysician and theologian.[18]

However, such a unified picture would hardly represent an adequate account of academic culture. In effect it ignores important features which an alternating model of secularisation and de-secularisation would have to take into account. It is quite clear that positivism has never convinced the entire non-theological academic community. Indeed, whilst positivism and behaviourism continue to play an important role within many disciplines, reactions against positivism and behaviourism are apparent too. So the functionalism of Malinowski within social anthropology is counterbalanced by the structuralism of Lévi-Strauss, and positivism within linguistics is attacked by Chomsky. Even within psychology, perhaps the most behaviourist social science discipline remaining, there is current opposition to the behaviourism of Skinner and Eysenck.[19]

Even if this opposition to positivism and behaviourism were not apparent within the academic community it would be possible to employ an alternating model. So. for example, it might be possible to argue that positivism does not create a situation of desacralisation at all. Rather it frees theology to concentrate on its own subject matter, using its own methodology and impinging on the rest of the academic community only at those points at which it has genuinely something to offer. Such a situation might well be interpreted in terms of de-secularisation. An alternating model of secularisation and de-secularisation at least allows for this possibility, as indeed it allows for the inevitable ambiguity of academic culture as a whole. It leaves open, however, the question of whether or not either secularisation or de-secularisation is increasing at the expense of the other.

A second example might be taken from the belief dimension of popular individual religiosity. A *prima facie* case can be made out for a process of secularisation in this dimension in the West, given most understandings of a substantive/exclusive definition of religion. Many surveys within both Britain[20] and the States[21] have indicated that the majority of the population today are not certain of their belief in traditional Christian doctrines. It seems reasonable to suppose that in the Middle Ages, at least, such certainty would have been far more widespread. It may or may not have been correlated with a high level of Christian activity, but probably it was higher than it is today. On this narrow definition, it seems that there has indeed been a process of secularisation apparent within the West.

Nevertheless, even this *prima facie* case is not without contradictions. Many sociologists have pointed out that there is also evidence for the rise in the West, for example, of belief in astrology and horoscopes.[22] Most substantive/exclusive definitions would have to take such evidences seriously as indeed referring to religious phenomena. Such evidence convinced Alasdair MacIntyre that secularisation was not in fact an accomplished fact in the West:

> Between the 10 per cent or so of clear and convinced Christians at one end of the scale and the 10 per cent or so of convinced sceptics at the other, there is the vast mass of the population, mostly superstitious to some degree, using the churches and especially the Church of England to celebrate birth, marriage, and death, and to a lesser degree Christmas. This use or misuse of the churches is rooted in a set of vague, half-formulated and inconsistent beliefs.[23]

Even without these contra-indications, however, it would still be possible to employ an alternating model of secularisation and de-secularisation. It has already been seen in the context of both Greeley and Yinger that a decline in the certainty of people's belief in traditional Christian doctrines can equally be interpreted in terms of de-secularisation. For Yinger the opposite thesis rests on a static rather than dynamic concept of religious belief, whereas for Greeley a situation of religious pluralism ensures that those who do believe in Christian doctrines do so out of choice and with conviction.

In both these examples an alternating model allows for the sheer complexity and ambiguity of the situation. A linear, uniform model—whether that of secularisation, de-secularisation or persistence—could only ignore this ambiguity and thereby distort the evidence. An alternating model based on the principle of complementarity, however, allows the sociologist to take account of a multi-faceted situation, without any pressure to make this situation conform to an overall 'historical sweep'.

The Implications of an Alternating Model for Theology

It remains to show how this alternating model might be applied to the specific area of the social context of theology. Undoubtedly it will prove considerably more complex than a single, uniform model. Nevertheless, two important consequences for theology derive from its use—the one negative and the other positive.

The negative consequence is straightforward but iconoclastic: sweeping historical models are unlikely to provide a satisfactory basis for the context of theology. This consequence is iconoclastic precisely because so much of contemporary theology has in fact been based on such models. So, for example, the evolutionary social model continues to play an important role amongst both contemporary followers of Teilhard de Chardin and proponents of 'process' theology. Amongst sociologists few today might oppose an overtly evolutionary social model—however much they might do so implicitly. Yet amongst theologians the evolutionary model still persists with vigour. In addition, as I have argued in previous chapters, the secularisation model has also played an extremely important role within recent theology. This model too must become immediately suspect if an alternating model is to be adopted in the social context of theology.

The confusion that reliance upon a single historical model has wrought amongst theologians is well illustrated by the following quotation. After a brief survey of theological attitudes to the apparent phenomenon of secularisation, the authors concluded:

> In theological perspective, secularisation seems a paradoxical affair indeed. Christian faith seems to constrain its adherents to be skeptical of secularisation precisely because the whole phenomena is *too* hospitable to religion, and especially to forms of religion that are particularly vicious because they are so often covert rather than acknowledged. On the other hand, Christian faith seems to constrain its adherents to be skeptical of secularisation precisely because it is *not* hospitable to the forms of religion that Christians may require for the deciphering of the contemporary divine work. Now would be a poor hour to lose the code, as the Lord struggles for and with man to preserve the fragile and precarious humanity of man—imperiled by business, by noisiness, by the decline of reflection, and especially by the quantification of time, the privatisation of freedom, and (Can one wonder or blame?) the loss of a sense of the cosmic.[24]

If an alternating model is adopted, one need make no evaluative response either for or against a process of secularisation, since the latter is no longer regarded as a linear historical process. A far more sophisticated response becomes necessary if Western religious phenomena are to be interpreted in terms of alternating processes or secularisation and de-secularisation.

This point leads naturally to the positive consequences of an alternating model for theology. Just as the principle of complementarity may be used internally within the sociology of religion, it is possible that it may also be used externally in relation to apparently contradictory methodologies. I argued in Part I that the sociologist is committed to an 'as if' methodology: in the specific instance of religion he is committed to the methodological assumption that there are social determinants of all religious phenomena, even if he is at present unable to specify all these determinants with accuracy. This is not an imperialistic claim for the sociological perspective: it is guarded against positivism or social determinism precisely because it is an 'as if' methodology. It is the sociologist's role to apply social explanations to religious phenomena quite relentlessly—and *not* psychological, or even theological, explanations. This method does not deny, though, that the latter may still be relevant to religion.

The notion of complementary methodologies is crucial in other spheres too. So, for example, it is fundamental to the Gestalt school of psychology. R. D. Laing offers the following example:

> Now if you are sitting opposite me, I can see you as another person like myself; without *you* changing or doing anything differently, I can now see you as a complex physical-chemical system, perhaps with its own idiosyncracies but chemical none the less for that; seen in this way, you are no longer a person but an organism. Expressed in the language of existential phenomenology, the other, as seen as a person or as seen as an organism, is the subject of different intentional acts. There is no dualism in the sense of the co-existence of two different essences or substances there in the object, psyche and soma; there are two different experiential Gestalts: person and organism.[25]

In theology, too, the notion of complementary methodologies may be important. In Chapter 3 I argued that, if the sociologist is committed to an 'as if' methodology of social determinism, the theologian is committed to an 'as if' methodology of transcendent causality. The latter, of course, is not obliged to maintain that only explanations of phenomena in terms of a system of transcendent causality are legitimate—such a claim would amount to the sort of theological imperialism characteristic of previous generations. But he is obliged to take seriously the notion of transcendence.

A similar argument is proposed by Maurice Wiles. He suggests that the theologian approaching the doctrine of creation is obliged to employ 'two stories'—the one scientific-historical and the other mythological:

> On the one hand we tell the scientific story of evolution; it is the real world as it has developed with which the doctrine of creation is concerned, not with some ideal world of the theological imagination. But in addition we tell a frankly mythological story about the spirit of God moving on the face of the chaotic waters, about God taking the dust of the earth, making

man in his own image, and breathing upon him so that he becomes a living soul. If we know what we are doing we can weave the two stories together in poetically creative ways—as indeed the poet combines logically disparate images into new and illuminating wholes. But we don't try to bind the two stories together at some specific point, claiming divine action to be at work in a special sense in the emergence of a first man with a distinct spiritual soul.[26]

Wiles' depiction of the theologian's task in terms of 'mythology' may or may not be satisfactory.[27] Yet his main point remains. It is important to maintain that the theologian's methodology is complementary, not in opposition, to scientific methodology.

The same phenomena that are of interest to the sociologist employing an alternating model of secularisation and de-secularisation are also of interest to the theologian, though for different reasons. Whereas the sociologist in some sense may attempt to be value-free (though doubtless unsuccessfully), the theologian is overtly value-oriented. So, for example, the phenomenon which the sociologist identifies as 'religiosity' is interpreted by the theologian in terms of 'faith.' The former is rightly concerned with attempting to quantify 'religiosity', but the latter is unlikely to feel happy about a quantification of 'faith'. The notions of 'religiosity' and 'faith' are not entirely unrelated when applied to the individual, though they do emanate from entirely different methodologies.

To pursue this example further, the two pit-falls that have been noted in previous chapters must be avoided. It is tempting, perhaps, for the theologian to conflate notions of 'religiosity' with those of 'faith'. Yet that would be to confuse sociological descriptions with theological prescriptions—since the theological notion of 'faith' contains important, but non-sociological, connotations connected with religious values. In addition, on an alternating model, it would be to oversimplify the specifically sociological analysis of 'religiosity'—itself a much broader concept than individual 'faith'. It is tempting again for the theologian to compensate for the deficiencies of purely sociological attempts to quantify religiosity. In Chapter 7 I argued that such attempts at quantification have as yet been comparatively unsuccessful. Nevertheless, apparent deficiencies within the sociological perspective cannot be legitimately remedied from outside that perspective—not, at least, without conflating sociology and theology.

The theologian cannot ignore the social context within which he works—even if he passes judgement on it and shares few contemporary plausibility structures. In so far as he investigates these plausibility structures he should employ the analyses provided by sociologists of religion. Nevertheless, he is not thereafter committed to a sociological perspective: his own theological perspective is complementary to, and not an extension of, this perspective. Even when the theologian is handling the same phenomena as the sociologist, his perspective is different. So, in the particular example of alternating processes of secularisation and de-secularisation, the theologian is prepared to make legitimate, evaluative interpretations in a way that the sociologist is not.

Theology in Context

In a brief, but important, postscript to his *The Invisible Religion* Thomas Luckmann provides a partial example of the method I am proposing for the theologian confronted with a sociological analysis of religious phenomena. Abandoning his sociological 'attitude of detachment', Luckmann makes an evaluative response to the findings of his own analysis of contemporary religion in the West. He does this precisely because he realises that this analysis 'touches upon matters of personal concern to everyone'.[28]

Luckmann's specifically sociological analysis has created a paradox; within contemporary Western society autonomy has been created for both its primary social institutions and its individual citizens. For the latter religion has increasingly been relegated to the 'private sphere': for the former religion has increasingly ceased to be significant:

> The discrepancy between the subjective 'autonomy' of the individual in modern society and the objective autonomy of the primary institutional domains strikes us as critical. The primary social institutions have 'emigrated' from the sacred cosmos. Their functional rationality is not part of a system that could be of 'ultimate' significance to the individuals in the society. This removes from the primary institutions much of the (potentially

135

intolerant) human pathos that proved to be fateful all too often in human history. If the process could be viewed in isolation it could justifiably appear as an essential component in freeing social arrangements from primitive emotions. The increasing autonomy of the primary institutions, however, has consequences for the relation of the individual to the social order—and thus, ultimately, to himself. Reviewing some of these consequences one is equally justified in describing this process as a process of dehumanisation of the basic structural components of the social order. The functional rationality of the primary social institutions seems to reinforce the isolation of the individual from his society, contributing thereby to the precariousness inherent in all social orders. Autonomy of the primary institutions, 'subjective' autonomy and *anomie* of the social order are dialectically related. At the very least it may be said that 'subjective' autonomy and autonomy of the primary institutions, the two most remarkable characteristics of modern industrial societies, are genuinely ambivalent phenomena.[29]

This evaluative response of Luckmann to his own sociological analysis is illuminating—however one ultimately assesses the details of this response or the analysis. In the first place it is clear that it is based on a thorough sociological analysis which takes into account the ambiguity of religious phenomena. And in the second place it is only suggested after, and *not* as a part of, the analysis. Luckmann, then, is careful not to interpret religious phenomena in terms of a linear model, and not to confuse essentially different methodologies. A theologian might well wish to go beyond his simple evaluative response, but he would do well to note the path by which Luckmann comes to it.

It is only by a long and painful path that the theologian can provide an adequate socio-theological correlation. The theologian, even as a theologian, is obliged to make certain assumptions about the society in which he is placed. If he fails to do so he may cease to communicate to that society. But if he attempts to do so he is faced with numerous difficulties. It has been the aim of this book to explore some of these difficulties.

Notes

CHAPTER 1

1. Peter Berger, *The Social Reality of Religion*, Faber & Faber, 1969, Appendix II, and *A Rumour of Angels*, Pelican, 1969.
2. David Martin, *The Religious and the Secular*, Routledge & Kegan Paul, 1969, and *Tracts Against the Times*, Lutterworth, 1973.
3. Ernst Troeltsch, *The Social Teaching of the Christian Churches*, Vols I and II, Harper, 1960.
4. Roland Robertson, *The Sociological Interpretation of Religion*, Blackwell, 1970.
5. Bryan Wilson, 'A Typology of Sects', in ed. Roland Robertson, *Sociology of Religion*, Penguin, 1969, and *Magic and the Millenium*, Heinemann, 1973.
6. Nicholas J. Demerath III, 'In a Sow's Ear: a Reply to Goode', *Journal for the Scientific Study of Religion*, Vol. VI, No. 1, 1967.
7. J. Milton Yinger, *Religion, Society and the Individual*, Macmillan, 1957, p. 9.
8. *ibid.*
9. H. D. Lewis, *Philosophy of Religion*, EUP, 1965, p. 127.
10. *ibid.*
11. Betty Scharf, *The Sociological Study of Religion*, Hutchinson, 1970. p. 33.
12. e.g. Alasdair MacIntyre, *A Short History of Ethics*, Routledge & Kegan Paul, 1967; Maria Ossowska, *Social Determinants of Moral Ideas*, Routledge & Kegan Paul, 1971; and John H. Barnsley, *The Social Reality of Ethics*, Routledge & Kegan Paul, 1972.
13. e.g. Michael Argyle, *Religious Behaviour*, Routledge & Kegan Paul, 1958.
14. Berger, *The Social Reality of Religion op. cit.* pp. 182–3.
15. cf. John Bowden, *Karl Barth*, SCM 1971.
16. Troeltsch, *op. cit.*
17. Werner Stark, *The Sociology of Religion*, Vols I–III, Routledge & Kegan Paul, 1966–7.
18. *ibid.* Vol. II, p. 5.
19. Wilson, *op. cit.* pp. 363–4.
20. Bryan Wilson, *Religion in Secular Society*, Pelican, 1969.
21. Max Weber, *The Sociology of Religion*, Methuen, 1965, p. 23.
22. Robin Gill, 'British Theology as a Sociological Variable', in ed. Michael Hill, *A Sociological Yearbook of Religion in Britain*, SCM, 1974.
23. Scharf, *op. cit.* pp. 132f.
24. Max Weber, *The Protestant Ethic and the Spirit of Capitalism*, Scribner, 1958, p. 91.
25. cf. Gary D. Bouma, 'Recent "Protestant Ethic" Research', *Journal for the Scientific Study of Religion*, Vol. 21, No. 2, 1973.
26. Gerhard E. Lenski, *The Religious Factor*, Doubleday, 1961.

27. Bouma, *op. cit.* p. 152.
28. Charles Y. Glock and Rodney Stark, *Christian Beliefs and Anti-Semitism*, Harper, 1966, pp. 94–5.
29. Dean R. Hoge & Jackson W. Carroll, 'Religiosity and Prejudice North and South', *Journal for the Scientific Study of Religion*, Vol. 12, No. 2, 1973: though see Richard L. Gorsuch and Daniel Aleshire, 'Christian Faith and Prejudice: 'Review of Research', *Journal for the Scientific Study of Religion*, Vol. 13, No. 3, 1974.
30. Roderick Martin, 'Sociology and Theology', in ed. D. E. H. Whitley and R. Martin, *Sociology, Theology and Conflict*, Blackwell, 1969, p. 34.
31. *ibid.* p. 36.
32. Ferdinand Boulard, *An Introduction to Religious Sociology*, Darton, Longman & Todd, 1960, p. 74.
33. *ibid.*

CHAPTER 2

1. cf. M. J. Jackson, 'Introduction to the English Edition', in F. Boulard, *An Introduction to Religious Sociology*, Darton, Longman & Todd, 1960, p.x.
2. cf. Thomas Luckmann, *The Invisible Religion*, Macmillan, 1967, p. 115.
3. cf. Michael Argyle, *Religious Behaviour*, Routledge & Kegan Paul, 1958, p. 1.
4. Michael Hill, *A Sociology of Religion*, Heinemann, 1973, p. 3.
5. Benjamin Nelson, 'Is the Sociology of Religion Possible? A Reply to Robert Bellah', *Journal for the Scientific Study of Religion*, Vol. 9, No. 2, 1970.
6. cf. Peter L. Berger, *The Social Reality of Religion*, Faber & Faber, 1969.
7. cf. Peter L. Berger, *A Rumour of Angels*, Pelican, 1969.
8. cf. Kenneth A. Thompson, *Bureaucracy and Church Reform*, OUP, 1970.
9. Boulard, *op. cit.*
10. J. H. Fichter, *Social Relations in the Urban Parish*, Chicago University Press, 1954.
11. Leslie Paul, *The Deployment and Payment of the Clergy*, Church of England Information Office, 1964, p. 11.
12. Margaret Hewitt, 'A Sociological Critique', in ed. F. G. Duffield, *The Paul Report Considered*, Marcham Manor Press, 1964.
13. Leslie Paul, 'The Role of the Clergy Today—An Organisational Approach: Problems of Deployment', in ed. C. L. Mitton, *The Social Sciences and the Churches*, T. &. T Clark, 1972, p. 170.
14. Eric Treacy, 'Approaching the Report', in ed. Duffield, *op. cit.*, p. 9.
15. *ibid.*, p. 10.
16. cf. Paul, *op. cit.* p. 171.
17. Boulard, *op. cit.*
18. John D. Gay, *The Geography of Religion in England*, Duckworth, 1971.
19. Robin Gill, 'Berger's Plausibility Structures: A Response to Professor Cairns', *Scottish Journal of Theology*, Vol. 27, No. 2, 1974.
20. Robin Gill, 'British Theology as a Sociological Variable', in ed. Michael Hill, *A Sociological Yearbook of Religion in Britain*, SCM, 1974.

138

21. cf. John Rex, *Key Problems of Sociological Theory*, Routledge & Kegan Paul, 1961, pp. vii f.
22. cf. David Martin, *The Religious and the Secular*, Routledge & Kegan Paul, 1969.
23. cf. Rex., *op. cit.* chap. 1.
24. cf. Ian G. Barbour, *Issues in Science and Religion*, SCM, 1966, pp. 137 f.
25. cf. Percy S. Cohen, *Modern Social Theory*, Heinemann, 1968, chap. 9.
26. Ninian Smart, *The Phenomenon of Religion*, Macmillan, 1973, p. 17.
27. Boulard, *op. cit.* p. 73.
28. *ibid.*

CHAPTER 3

1. John Bowker, *The Sense of God*, OUP, 1973, p. 181.
2. *ibid.* pp. 181–2.
3. *ibid.* pp. 121–2.
4. *ibid.* p. 34.
5. Peter L. Berger, *The Social Reality of Religion*, Faber & Faber, 1969, p. 26.
6. Bowker, *op. cit.* pp. 35–6.
7. Berger, *op. cit.* p. 193 n. 34.
8. *ibid.* p. 181.
9. *ibid.* p. 14.
10. see Robin Gill, 'Berger's Plausibility Structures: A Response to Professor Cairns', *Scottish Journal of Theology*, Vol. 27, No. 2, 1974.
11. Berger, *op. cit.* p. 106.
12. cf. Liam Hudson, *The Cult of the Fact*, Jonathan Cape, 1972.
13. John Rex, *Key Problems of Sociological Theory*, Routledge & Kegan Paul, 1961, p. 25.
14. Ninian Smart, *The Phenomenon of Religion*, Macmillan, 1973, p. 59.
15. Ian Hamnett, 'Sociology of Religion and Sociology of Error', *Religion* Spring 1973, Vol. 3, p. 3.
16. Robert Towler, *Homo Religiosus; Sociological Problems in the Study of Religion*, Constable, 1974, p. 2.
17. *ibid.*
18. Robert N. Bellah, *Beyond Belief*, Harper & Row, 1970, p. 247.
19. *ibid.* p. 248.
20. *ibid.* p. 249.
21. *ibid.* p. 240.
22. *ibid.* pp. 245–6.
23. cf. Hudson, *op. cit.*
24. cf. Max Black, *Models and Metaphors*, Cornell University Press, 1962.
25. cf. Ian G. Barbour, *Issues in Science and Religion*, SCM, 1966.
26. cf. Ian T. Ramsey, *Religious Language*, SCM, 1959.
27. Bellah, *op. cit.* p. 253.
28. *ibid.* p. 257.
29. *ibid.* p. 195.
30. Thomas Robbins, Dick Anthony and Thomas E. Curtis, 'The Limits of Symbolic Realism', *Journal for the Scientific Study fo Religion*, Vol. 12, No. 3, 1973.
31. Ian Hogbin, *Social Change*, Watts, 1957, pp. 24f.
32. Edmund R. Leach, *Political Systems of Highland Burma*, London, 1954, p. 285.

33. Berger, *op. cit.* p. 12.
34. H. Vaihinger, *The Philosophy of 'As If'*, Kegan Paul, 1924, p. 15.

CHAPTER 4

1. cf. David B. Harned, *The Ambiguity of Religion*, Westminster Press, 1968.
2. cf. Harvey Cox, 'The Prophetic Purpose of Theology', in ed. Dean Peerman, *Frontline Theology*, 1967.
3. cf. Harned, *op. cit.*
4. Harvey Cox, *The Secular City*, Pelican, 1968, p. 52.
5. *ibid.* p. 53.
6. *ibid.* p. 59.
7. R. H. Pahl, *Patterns of Urban Living*, Longman, 1970, p. 136.
8. David B. Harned, *Grace and Common Life*, University of Virginia, 1970, chap. 5, and *Faith and Virtue*, St. Andrews, 1973, chap. 1.
9. David B. Harned, *Theology and the Arts*, Westminster Press, 1966, pp. 24–5.
10. John Ferguson, 'The Secular City Revisited', *The Modern Churchman*, April 1973, p. 191.
11. cf. David Shepherd, *Built as a City*, Hodder & Stoughton, 1974, pp. 18–19.
12. Cox, *op. cit.* p. 59.
13. Paul van Buren, *The Secular Meaning of the Gospel*, SCM, 1963.
14. Peter Rudge, *Ministry and Management*, Tavistock, 1969.
15. J. A. T. Robinson, *The Human Face of God*, SCM, 1973, pp. 20–1.
16. *ibid.* pp. 21–2.
17. *ibid.* p. 23.
18. e.g. Peter L. Berger, *A Rumour of Angels*, Pelican, 1969 and Bryan Wilson, *Religion in Secular Socitey*, Pelican, 1969.
19. cf. David Martin, 'The Secularisation Question', *Theology*, Feb. 1973.
20. Robinson, *op. cit.* p. 27.
21. David Martin, 'Ethical Commentary and Political Decision', *Theology*, Oct. 1973, p. 527.
22. cf. R.C. Zaehner, *Drugs, Mysticism and Make-Believe*, Collins, 1972, p. 29, and Andrew M. Greeley, *Priests in the United States—Reflections on a Survey*, Doubleday, 1972, p. 13.

CHAPTER 5

1. e.g. E.L. Mascall, *The Secularisation of Christianity*, Libra, 1967, and R. Holloway, *Let God Arise*, Mowbrays, 1972.
2. Mascall, *op. cit.* p. 6.
3. *ibid.* p. 7.
4. *ibid.* p. 8.
5. E.L. Mascall, *Theology and Images*, Mowbrays, 1963.
6. Peter L. Berger, *A Rumour of Angels*, Pelican, 1969, pp. 54–5.
7. *Religion in Britain and Northern Ireland*, Independent Television Authority, 1970, p. 19.
8. cf. articles on 'The LAM Religiosity Scale', Andrew M. Greeley, *et al.* in *Journal for the Scientific Study of Religion*, Vol. 12, Nos. 1–3 1973.

9. Albert Maori Kiki, *Kiki—Ten Thousand Years in a Lifetime*, Cheshire, 1968, p. 52.
10. Berger, *op. cit.* p. 18.
11. *ibid.* p. 30.
12. *ibid.* p. 18.
13. *ibid.* pp. 18–19.
14. Peter L. Berger, *The Precarious Vision*, Doubleday, 1961.
15. Berger, *A Rumour of Angels*, *op. cit.* p. 59.
16. cf. David Cairns, 'Peter Berger' *Scottish Journal of Theology*, Vol. 27, No. 2, 1974.
17. cf. Cairns, *op. cit.* and Robin Gill, 'Berger's Plausibility Structures: A Response to Professor Cairns', *Scottish Journal of Theology*, Vol. 27, No. 2, 1974.
18. cf. Thomas Robbins, Dick Anthony and Thomas E. Curtis, 'The Limits of Symbolic Realism', *Journal for the Scientific Study of Religion*, Vol. 12, No. 3, 1973.
19. Leonard Hodgson, *For Faith and Freedom*, Blackwell, Vol. 1, 1956, pp. 13–14.
20. Karl Rahner, *Theological Investigations*, Vol. 1, Darton, Longman & Todd, 1961, p. 150.
21. cf. Friedrich Schumann, 'Can the Event of Jesus Christ Be Demythologised?', in ed. H. V. Bartsch, *Kerygma and Myth*, Vol. 1, SPCK, 1953, and H. P. Owen, *Revelation and Existence*, Cardiff, 1957, pp. 6f.
22. Rudolf Bultmann in ed. Bartsch, *op. cit.* p. 10.
23. *ibid.*
24. e.g. Helmut Thielicke, in ed. Bartsch, *op. cit.* pp. 142f., and G. Vaughan Jones, *Christology and Myth in the New Testament*, London, 1957, pp. 6f.
25. e.g. Bultmann, *op. cit.* pp. 196f.
26. Paul van Buren, *The Secular Meaning of the Gospel*, SCM, 1963.
27. Paul van Buren, interview in *New Christian*, 25 July, 1968, pp. 12–13.

CHAPTER 6

1. Robin Gill, 'British Theology as a Sociological Variable', in ed. Michael Hill, *A Sociological Yearbook of Religion in Britain*, SCM, 1974.
2. cf. James F. Childress and David B. Harned, *Secularisation and the Protestant Prospect*, Westminster, 1970.
3. C. Y. Glock and C. R. Stark, *American Piety: The Nature of Religious Commitment*, University of California Press, 1968, pp. 11–19.
4. *ibid.*
5. Roland Robertson, *The Sociological Interpretation of Religion* Blackwell, 1969, pp. 53.
6. *ibid.* cf. Robert Towler, *Homo Religiosus: Sociological Problems in the Study of Religion*, Constable, 1974, p. 131.
7. cf. C. Y. Glock and C. R. Stark, *Christian Beliefs and Anti-Semitism*, Harper, 1966.
8. Robertson, *op. cit.* p. 56.
9. *ibid.* p. 57.
10. *ibid.*
11. *ibid.* p. 59.

12. J.A.T. Robinson, *Honest to God*, SCM, 1963.
13. Robinson in ed. J. A. T. Robinson and D. Edwards, *The Honest to God Debate*, SCM, 1963, p. 248.
14. *ibid.* p. 249.
15. *ibid.* pp. 249f.
16. *ibid.* p. 253.
17. *ibid.* p. 252.
18. *ibid.*
19. *ibid.* p. 268.
20. *ibid.* pp. 268–9.
21. E. L. Mascall, *The Secularisation of Christianity*, Darton, Longman & Todd, 1965, p. 7.
22. *ibid.* p. 35.
23. *ibid.* p. 44.
24. A. M. Ramsey, *God, Christ and the World*, SCM, 1969, p. 17.
25. *ibid.* p. 16.
26. *ibid.*
27. *ibid.*
28. *ibid.* p. 27.
29. Leslie Newbigin, *Religion for Secular Man*, SCM, 1966, p. 11.
30. *ibid.*
31. *ibid.* p. 12.
32. *ibid.*
33. *ibid.* p. 13.
34. *ibid.* pp. 13–14.
35. *ibid.*
36. *ibid.* p. 14.
37. *ibid* p. 15.
38. *ibid.* 17.
39. F.R. Barry, *Secular and Supernatural*, SCM, 1969, p. 19.
40. Mass Observation, *Puzzled People*, 1948.
41. Barry, *op. cit.* p. 22.
42. *ibid.* p. 30.

CHAPTER 7

1. Marshall McLuhan, *The Medium is the Message*, Penguin, 1967.
2. ed. G. M. Stearn, *McLuhan Hot and Cool*, Penguin, 1968, and Jonathan Miller, *McLuhan*, Fontana, 1971.
3. see J. D. Halloran, *The Effects of Mass Communications*, Leicester University Press, 1964.
4. Alasdair MacIntyre, *Marcuse*, Fontana, 1970, p. 17.
5. Peter L. Berger, *A Rumour of Angels*, Pelican, 1969, p. 18.
6. Peter L. Berger, *The Social Reality of Religion*, Faber & Faber, 1969, p. 113.
7. *ibid.* p. 34.
8. *ibid.* p. 114.
9. John Bowker, *The Sense of God*, OUP, 1973, p. 122.
10. F. Boulard, *An Introduction to Religious Sociology*, Darton, Longman & Todd, 1960.
11. see John D. Gay, *The Geography of Religion in England*, Duckworth, 1971.

12. cf. Robert Towler, *Homo Religiosus: Sociological Problems in the Study of Religion.* Constable, 1974, p. 131.
13. Boulard, *op. cit.* p. 3, cf. Towler, *op. cit.* p. 7.
14. Independent Television Authority, *Religion in Britain and Northern Ireland*, ITA Publication, 1970.
15. *ibid.* p. 53.
16. *ibid.*
17. *ibid.*
18. *ibid.*
19. e.g. Charles Y. Glock and Rodney Stark, *American Piety*, Harper & Row, 1969, cf. Geoffrey K. Nelson and Rosemary A. Clews, *Mobility and Religious Commitment*, University of Birmingham Institute for the Study of Worship and Religious Architecture, 1971.
20. see Charles Y. Glock and Rodney Stark, *Christian Beliefs and Anti-Semitism*, Harper and Row, 1966.
21. R. Robertson and C. Campbell, 'Religion in Britain: the Need for New Research Strategies', *Social Compass*, XIX/2, 1972, p. 197.
22. Berger, *Social Reality, op. cit.*, p. 115 cf. Thomas F. O'Dea, *The Sociology of Religion*, Prentice-Hall, 1966, pp. 72f.
23. *ibid.* p. 116.
24. *ibid.* p. 117.
25. *ibid.* p. 121.
26. *ibid.* p. 126.
27. Bryan Wilson, *Religion in Secular Society*, Pelican, 1969.
28. *ibid.* p. 9.
29. *ibid.* p. 10.
30. *ibid.* p. 12.
31. Bryan Wilson, *Magic and the Millennium*, Heinemann, 1973, p. 504.
32. Thomas Luckmann, *The Invisible Religion*, Collier-Macmillan, 1967, p. 22.
33. *ibid.* p. 23.
34. Wilson, *Religion in Secular Society, op. cit.*, p. 25.
35. Robert Bocock, *Ritual in Industrial Society*, George Allen & Unwin, 1974, p. 71.
36. Peter L. Berger, forward to *Zur Dialektik von Religion und Gesellschaft*, (German edit. of *Social Reality*), S. Fischer Verlag, 1973.
37. Peter L. Berger, Brigitte Berger and Hansfried Kellner, *The Homeless Mind*, Pelican, 1974, p. 15.
38. Luckmann, *op. cit.*
39. Berger *et al.*, *op. cit.*, p. 76.
40. Talcott Parsons, *Sociological Theory and Modern Society*, Free Press, 1967.
41. Berger *et al.*, *op. cit.*, p. 12.
42. Wilson, *op. cit.*, pp. 47–8.
43. *ibid.* p. 44.
44. cf. Parsons, *op. cit.*
45. Michael Hill, *The Religious Order*, Heinemann, 1973, p. 3.
46. Wilson, *op. cit.*, pp. 51–2.
47. cited in Glock and Stock, *Anti-Semitism, op. cit.*, p. 81.
48. Bryan S. Turner, 'The Sociological Explanation of Ecumenicalism', in ed. C. L. Mitton, *The Social Sciences and the Churches*, T. & T. Clark, 1972.
49. Wilson, *op. cit.*, p. 152.

50. Peter L. Berger, 'A Market Model for the Analysis of Ecumenicity', *Social Research*, Spring 1963, pp. 77f.
51. Robin Gill, 'British Theology as a Sociological Variable', in ed. Michael Hill, *A Sociological Yearbook of Religion in Britain*, SCM, 1974.
52. see J. H. S. Burleigh, *A Church History of Scotland*, OUP, 1960.

CHAPTER 8

1. David Martin, *The Religious and the Secular*, Routledge & Kegan Paul, 1969, p. 22.
2. *ibid.* pp. 9–22.
3. *ibid.* p. 22.
4. Peter L. Berger, *The Social Reality of Religion*, Faber & Faber, 1969, p. 112.
5. *ibid.* p. 209, n.7.
6. David Martin, 'The Secularisation Question', *Theology*, LXXVI, No. 630, Feb. 1973, p. 82.
7. *ibid.* pp. 81–2.
8. e.g. Gerhard Lenski, *The Religious Factor*, Anchor, 1963. cf. Jan Lauwers, 'Les théories sociologiques concernant le sécularisation—Typologie et critique', *Social Compass*, XX/4, 1973.
9. Martin, *The Religious and the Secular, op. cit.*, p. 11.
10. *ibid.* p. 12.
11. *ibid.*
12. e.g. Betty R. Scharf, *The Sociological Study of Religion*, Hutchinson, 1970, pp. 35f, E. Krausz, 'Religion and Secularisation. A Matter of Definition', *Social Compass*, XVIII/2, 1971, and Karel Dobbelaere and Jan Lauwers, 'Definitions of Religion—a Sociological Critique', *Social Compass*, XX/4, 1973.
13. J. M. Yinger, 'Pluralism, Religion and Secularism', *Journal for the Scientific Study of Religion*, VI, No. 1, 1967, p. 18.
14. John Bowker, *The Sense of God*, OUP, 1973, p. 181.
15. J. M. Yinger, *Sociology Looks at Religion*, Macmillan, 1963, pp. 72f.
16. e.g. Scharf, *op. cit.* p. 32, and Dobbelaere and Lauwers, *op. cit.* p. 537.
17. E. Durkheim, *Elementary Forms of Religious Life*, 1964, ed., p. 47.
18. E. B. Tylor, *Primitive Culture*, 1871.
19. Roland Robertson, *The Sociological Interpretation of Religion*, Blackwell, 1970, p. 47.
20. *ibid.* pp. 235f.
21. e.g. Krausz, *op. cit.*
22. John Rex, *Race Relations in Sociological Theory*, Weidenfeld & Nicolson, 1970.
23. e.g. Louis Schneider, *Sociological Approach to Religion*, Wiley, 1970, pp. 176f, and Lauwers, *op. cit.* pp. 524–9.
24. Larry Shiner, 'The Meanings of Secularisation', *International Yearbook for the Sociology of Religion*, Vol. III, 1967, re-printed in ed. James F. Childress and David B. Harned, *Secularisation and the Protestant Prospect*, Westminster, 1970.
25. *ibid.* p. 31.
26. *ibid.* p. 33.
27. *ibid.* p. 35.

28. *ibid.* p. 36.
29. *ibid.* p. 37.
30. *ibid.* p. 38.
31. cf. Peter N. Glasner, 'Secularisation: Its Limitations and Usefulness in Sociology', in ed. C. L. Mitton, *The Social Sciences and the Churches*, T. & T. Clark, 1972, p. 246–257, Michael Hill, *A Sociology of Religion*, Heinemann, 1973, pp. 228f.
32. Shiner, *op. cit.* p. 41.
33. *ibid.*
34. cf. Glasner, *op. cit.*, pp. 256–7.
35. S. Yeo, 'A study of Religion in Reading in the late Nineteenth and early Twentieth Centuries', Ph.D. thesis, Sussex University, 1972.
36. Martin in *Theology*, *op. cit.*, p. 86.
37. Andrew M. Greeley, *The Persistence of Religion*, SCM, 1973, p. 16.
38. *ibid.*
39. *ibid.* p. 14.
40. *ibid.*
41. *ibid.* p. 54.
42. cf. André de Neve, 'Secularisation in Russian Sociology of Religion', *Social Compass*, XX/4, 1973.
43. *ibid.* p. 36.
44. *ibid.* p. 36.
45. cf. J. Burrow, *Evolution and Society*, CUP, 1966.
46. cf. Robert N. Bellah, 'Religious Evolution', in ed. Roland Robertson, *Sociology of Religion*, Penguin, 1969.
47. Bowker, *op. cit.*, p. 57.
48. *ibid.* cf. Robert A. Nisbet, *Social Change and History*, OUP, 1969.
49. cf. Jeffrey K. Hadden and Patrick H. McNamara, 'Review Symposium: Andrew Greeley', *Journal for the Scientific Study of Religion*, Vol. 13, No. 1, March, 1974.

CHAPTER 9

1. David Martin, 'The Secularisation Question', *Theology*, LXXVI, No. 630, Feb. 1973, p. 86, cf. Mary Douglas, 'Heathen Darkness, Modern Piety', *New Society*, 12 March 1970.
2. Bryan Wilson, *Religion in Secular Society*, Pelican, 1969.
3. Bryan Wilson, *Sects and Society*, Heinemann, 1955.
4. cf. Peter Sissons, *The Social Significance of Church Membership in the Burgh of Falkirk*, Church of Scotland, 1973, pp. 74f.
5. cf. Roderick Martin, 'Sociology and Theology', in ed. D.E.H. Whitley and R. Martin, *Sociology, Theology and Conflict*, Blackwell, 1969.
6. Andrew M. Greeley, *The Persistence of Religion*, SCM, 1973, p. 15. cf. Talcott Parsons, *Sociological Theory and Modern Society*, Free Press, 1967.
7. J. Milton Yinger, *The Scientific Study of Religion*, Macmillan, 1970, pp. 488f.
8. J. Milton Yinger, *Sociology Looks at Religion*, Macmillan, 1963, p. 73.
9. Michael Hill, *The Religious Order*, Heinemann, 1973, p. 207.
10. *ibid.* pp. 207–8, cf. Parsons, *op. cit.*
11. *ibid.* p. 293.
12. Thomas Luckmann, *The Invisible Religion*, Macmillan, 1967.

13. Robert N. Bellah, 'Civil Religion in America', in ed. James F. Childress and David B. Harned, *Secularisation and the Protestant Prospect*, Westminster, 1970.
14. cf. K. Dobbelaere and J. Lauwers, 'Definitions of Religion—A Sociological Critique', *Social Compass*, XX/4, 1973.
15. Ian G. Barbour, *Issues in Science and Religion*, SCM, 1966, p. 157.
16. *ibid.* pp. 157–8.
17. Max Black, *Models and Metaphors*, Cornell University Press, 1962, p. 237.
18. cf. Roderick Martin, *op. cit.*
19. cf. Liam Hudson, *The Cult of the Fact*, Jonathan Cape, 1972.
20. e.g. Independent Television Authority, *Television and Religion*, ABC, 1965, and *Religion in Britain and Northern Ireland*, ITA, 1970.
21. e.g. Charles Y. Glock and Rodney Stark, *American Piety*, Harper & Row, 1969.
22. cf. David Martin, *A Sociology of English Religion*, Heinemann, 1967, and G. Jahoda, *The Psychology of Superstition*, Pelican, 1969.
23. Alasdair MacIntyre, in ed. D. Edwards and J.A.T. Robinson, *The Honest to God Debate*, SCM, 1963, p. 223.
24. Childress and Harned, *op. cit.*, p. 27.
25. R.D. Laing, *The Divided Self*, Pelican, 1965, p. 21.
26. M.F. Wiles, 'Does Christology Rest on a Mistake?', in ed. S.W. Sykes and J.P. Clayton, *Christ, Faith and History*, CUP, 1972, p. 8.
27. cf. Peter R. Baelz, 'A Deliberate Mistake?', in ed. Sykes and Clayton, *op .cit.*
28. Luckmann, *op. cit.*, p. 115.
29. *ibid.* pp. 115–16.

Author Index

147

148

Subject Index

149